RECIPES
from a
FRENCH
HERB GARDEN

RECIPES
from a
FRENCH
HERB GARDEN

GERALDENE HOLT

Special photography by
Linda Burgess

CONRAN OCTOPUS

For Mary Frances Kennedy Fisher,
with affection and gratitude.

I am indebted to many people, over many years, in both France and
England for the experience and wisdom that they have generously
given in the interests of good food.
For their help and encouragement with this book, I am
specially grateful to Yvette Marquet, Suzanne and Jeannette
Doize, Susan and Harry Beazley, Pamela Todd, Scott Ewing,
Jean Joice and Philippa Davenport.
Finally, it has been a tremendous pleasure to work with Linda
Burgess and her assistant, Debbie Patterson. Linda's photographs
never fail to summon up the happy and powerful association of
food with place.

All spoonfuls in the recipes are level unless otherwise stated.

First published in 1989 by
Conran Octopus Limited
37 Shelton Street
London WC2H 9HN

Project Editor – Cortina Butler
Art Director – Mary Evans
Designers – Kit Johnson, Meryl Lloyd
Picture Research – Nadine Bazar
Production – Shane Lask
Photographic Stylist – Deborah Patterson
Painted Plates – Lesley Harle
Line Artwork – Carol Wilhide
Editorial Assistant – Henrietta Gill

British Library Cataloguing in Publication Data

Holt, Geraldene
    Recipes from a French herb garden
    1. Food. French dishes using herbs.
    Recipes
    I. Title
    641.6′57′0944

ISBN 1-85029-176-4

Typeset by Elite Typesetting Techniques, Southampton
Printed and bound in Italy
Amilcare Pizzi S.p.a.

CONTENTS

INTRODUCTION

T̲ᴿᴬᵛᴱᴸᴸᴵᴺᴳ south through France, along the valley of the Rhône, there is always an exhilarating moment in the journey when I notice that the roof tiles have changed. Somewhere around Lyon, the deep-red tiles of the north give way to the sunbleached terracotta of the south.

When every town and village you pass through glows with the same orange tiles, you know that you have arrived in the Midi; in that region of France where the colonizing Roman legions felt so at home that they made it a province of their own country and called it *Provincia*. This is the region of France where herbs still grow wild on the hillsides, and the food, the wine, and the pace of life are all deeply influenced by the incandescence of the sun.

It was in a small village in northern Provence that I first discovered one of my favourite French herb gardens. Built into a ledge of the hillside and overlooking the flat valley of the Rhône far below, the garden is surrounded by a stone wall which offers good protection from the damaging mistral wind. The garden was once part of a medieval monastery, and even today medicinal herbs jostle for space alongside the tarragon and fennel, the parsley and thyme, among the culinary herbs.

As I walk in this ancient herb garden with its simple beauty, I sense, once again, the special quality to be found there which nearly every herb garden shares. There is a calmness about the garden, a peaceful atmosphere of harmony and warmth which is timeless. Being in this garden of scents and perfumes, of leaf pattern and flower, is a very personal pleasure, often best enjoyed alone. And yet, although I usually choose to be on my own in a herb garden, I never feel lonely. Herbs, it seems to me, are the most companionable of plants.

Herbs have grown wild in Provence since the earliest times. The rocky terrain, with patches of thin soil that support the low-growing *maquis* of shrubs and herbs, has remained unchanged for thousands of years. The powerful landscape has inspired writers and artists for generations: Mistral and Zola, Cézanne and Van Gogh, have all eloquently recorded this country that attracts like a magnet. For a few years Paul Cézanne tried to live and paint in the northern light of Paris, until, as he wrote, 'the sun dragged me back'.

It is the sun that makes Provençal herbs so particular. Observing how they grow wild in their natural habitat, it is instructive to see how little soil they need to survive. This apparent soil starvation and the hot, dry climate combine to make the herbs highly scented and flavourful. For me, these are the best of herbs. I pick them, cook with them and even grow my own herbs in England from seeds and cuttings brought back from holidays spent in France.

But not all the local cooks feel this way. When a friend in the Ardèche saw me picking wild thyme, known there as *serpolet* or *farigoule*, she declared that I couldn't possibly use those herbs in my cooking – she'd bring me some from her garden which tasted far better. I smiled and proceeded to cook with both my wild herbs and her lusher cultivated varieties. Neither was better, they were just different.

GARLIC FOR SALE *A familiar sight, when driving through the South of France in the summer months, is a sign outside one of the farms advertising vegetables or fruit for sale. A bunch of garlic illustrates this sign informing passers-by that garlic can be bought in the farmhouse.*

8

The herb garden is the oldest form of garden. Garden historians tell us that the earliest ones were built to a rectangular design and enclosed by a low earth bank to protect the tender plants from cold winds. At various points the wall was dug out to make an earthen bench which was planted with creeping herbs like chamomile and thyme, intended for sitting on. The herb beds were separated by narrow paths of carpeting herbs such as pennyroyal that sweetly perfumed the air when walked upon. It is clear that, from the beginning, a herb garden was intended to feed all the senses. For herbs delight the eye and the nose, the mouth and the hand, and no less the ear – as when a breeze rustles tall stalks of fennel or you hear the sound of bees busy gathering nectar from the flowers of a lavender bush.

Herbs have a long and distinguished role in the history of French food. They have figured in cooking since before the days of Charlemagne who, it is said, dined on

PROVENÇAL LUNCH *The large green leaves of a fig tree shade a family eating their midday meal. The stone courtyard of the old farmhouse near Uzès catches the sun that shines almost continuously in Provence from June until the winter.*

roast game stuffed with herbs. In the seventeenth century, the father of French agriculture Olivier de Serres listed forty different herbs to be grown in the well-organized kitchen garden. La Varenne includes many different herbs in his cookery book *Le Cuisinier François* published in 1651. The best French cooks of today would never contemplate cooking without fresh herbs, as many of the dishes of Bocuse, Guérard, Bras, Perrier and Vergé testify.

My closest friends in France are country people who cook with the produce of their own gardens and with provisions from a weekly trip to the local market. No meal is prepared without a sprig of parsley here or a bay leaf added to a dish there. Their kitchens are decorated with bundles of dried herbs – marjoram and oregano picked just as they come into flower, dark green lustrous bay leaves and the swelling bulbs of rose-flushed garlic. There might be a bowl of freshly picked juniper berries and a posy of *poivre d'âne* – ass's pepper – or wild savory. All these herbs are used freely and naturally in their good country cooking. The herbs are from their gardens, the fields and the surrounding hills. The food has a true *goût de terroir* which reflects the local ingredients.

Until recently I grew my herbs in a long straggly row next to the asparagus in my kitchen garden. It was an unplanned arrangement and it was far from ideal. The herbs were not close enough to the kitchen and I was also denied the pleasure of seeing them from the house. It was when I began to research and write this book that I decided this was the perfect time to move my herbs. So I have now built a small French-inspired garden, in the old farmyard behind our Devon farmhouse.

First of all I removed a large rectangle of turf. This revealed stony ground which should be ideal for growing herbs. But to give the plants a good start I covered the lightly forked soil with a thin layer of loam mixed with well-rotted compost. The design is simple, with cobbled paths dividing the garden into four beds that open out in the centre to make a round space large enough to place a sundial. The whole herb garden is surrounded by a cobbled path and lawn.

Planting up the garden has been immensely enjoyable – deciding which herbs should be included and where they should go. First of all, I planted some of the tall herbs such as angelica and lovage, fennel and lemon balm towards the middle of each bed. Medium-height herbs like tarragon, borage and dill, lavender, rosemary and sage were planted around them. And then the low-growing herbs like marjoram and basil went in nearest the paths. I planted many kinds of thyme around the sundial and used neat-growing herbs such as chives, hyssop, parsley and sorrel as edging around the beds.

In just a few months the herb garden is beginning to look well established and it is already a quiet, scented corner of the garden in which to sit or walk. On a sunny morning I take my first cup of coffee of the day there, and sit looking at the variety of shades of green and grey,

thinking about other people who, over the centuries, have been equally fascinated by these lovely plants. For herbs have changed remarkably little over the years – plant breeders have left most of them well alone. True, there are a few new varieties of rosemary and lavender, but I find it pleasing that gardeners and cooks of the past have grown and picked the very same plants that we do. It is a consoling and humbling thought.

Although I am now able to devote a fair amount of space to growing herbs, there have been times when I had no more room than a window-sill, and I grew all my herbs in pots. Most herbs relish this cossetted life, which, ideally, means spending the summer outside and being moved indoors at the first hint of cold weather.

Almost any pot is suitable for growing herbs: more important is the potting mixture and growing position – on the whole the sunniest site suits herbs best. But even if all you can offer your herbs is a shady backyard, take heart – a friend of mine grows huge clay pots of bright-green, crisp sorrel in a similar situation. Another friend prunes and shapes her pot-grown herbs until they re-semble a miniature topiary, and her tiny paved garden is made most attractive with a dozen or so of these doll's-house-size trees.

I was brought up to cook with herbs and I still do so, finding their study and use an absorbing interest. Knowing more about the herbs that have such an important place in the kitchen greatly increases the pleasure of both cooking and eating. It might be reasonable to reckon, though, that we already know all there is to know about herbs. But not so, almost everyday a plant scientist, a doctor of green medicine, a homeopath, a chef or even an amateur cook discovers some new aspect of these wonder plants that, increasingly, appear to be essential to our health and happiness.

Even if your experience of cooking with herbs has gone no further than buying a bunch of parsley or a small packet of chives from the supermarket, I hope that the following pages will inspire you to venture further into that realm of cooking whose fine flavour depends on these delightful plants.

Clyst William Barton,
Devon.

HERBS
FROM A FRENCH
GARDEN

*Herbs are lovingly cultivated
in gardens, pots and window-boxes
all over France – a reflection of
the central role that they
have played in French cuisine for
hundreds of years.*

TRADITIONAL PLANTING *The gardens of the Château de Bailleul have been recently restored using original designs of French Renaissance gardens. They contain many rare and ancient varieties of medicinal and culinary herbs.*

ANGELICA

ANGÉLIQUE

The fresh leaves of angelica are used in salads and to flavour compôtes of fresh fruit. The herb has a useful sweetening effect on tart fruit such as rhubarb, which means that less sugar is needed in cooking. The stems of angelica are crystallized to make a delightful flavouring for cakes, tarts and creams. Angelica is grown extensively in the Loire valley, and the towns of Nevers and Niort have become centres of the crystallizing industry. A liqueur flavoured with the herb and a gateau made with egg whites and crystallized angelica are specialities of the region.
CULTIVATION Hardy biennial. Grow in a rich, moist soil, in a sunny or in a partly shaded position. Encourage the growth of foliage by removing flower heads as they appear, and in any case, harvest leaves for drying before the midsummer flowering time.

ANISE

ANIS

The herb is mainly grown for its seed although its feathery leaves are delicious as part of a green salad. The dark green, dried seed is usually available on herb and spice stalls. Aniseed goes well with root vegetables but is more commonly used to flavour biscuits, in Alsace, and some rich breads, in Provence. The herb is the main flavouring in the aniseed-based aperitifs, like Pernod, that are diluted with water for drinking. Anisette is the French aniseed-based liqueur.
CULTIVATION Tender annual. Anise requires a hot climate for the

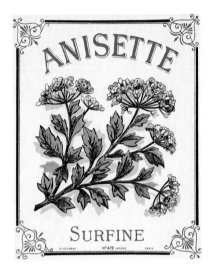

ANISE *The feathery green leaves and yellow flower heads of anise adorn a label for the French liqueur Anisette.*

seeds to ripen. To grow it for its fragrant leaves, however, sow seed in late spring in light soil and in a sunny sheltered position.

BASIL, SWEET BASIL

BASILIC COMMUN

A beautifully fragrant herb with a clove-like scent that is widely used in Provençal cooking. Only fresh basil is worth considering – it does not dry well – although, for use out of season, its flavour can be preserved in a herb butter, oil or vinegar. Basil is an essential ingredient of the Niçois version of Genoese pesto sauce, known as pistou. The herb is excellent in many salads and has a well-known affinity with tomatoes. Basil also goes well with chicken, lamb and some oily fish. French cooks use basil with a medium-sized leaf, although the Italian large-leaved basil and the Greek small-

leaved basil are both useful in cooking. The purple-leaved opal basil has less flavour but it is highly decorative in salads.
CULTIVATION Tender annual. Plant seeds in late spring in well-drained soil in a warm, sheltered position. Do not overwater. Use fresh pickings until autumn frosts. After picking large quantities, cut the plant back to encourage fresh growth.

BAY, SWEET BAY

LAURIER

The bay leaf has been described as the characteristic flavouring of French cooking. The fragrance of the leaf is slightly balsamic. The fresh leaf, which has a delicate balance of lemon and nutmeg, becomes spicier (and to my mind less subtle) as it dries. The flavour of a dried leaf is about twice as strong as a fresh one. Bay is used in all regions of France to flavour soups, sauces, and some sweet custards and creams. A bay leaf is one of the three herbs, with parsley and thyme, that make up the classic bouquet garni.
CULTIVATION Hardy evergreen shrub. Grow in a sunny, sheltered position. Protect young plants from cold winters. Once the shrub is established, leaves may be picked throughout the year.

BORAGE

BOURRACHE

A very decorative herb with dull-green hairy leaves and lovely bright blue flowers. The flowers of borage, which taste like cucumber, have been used to decorate salads from the early seventeenth century. Both the flowers and the leaves of borage are

dipped in batter and fried to make fritters. The young leaves are some-times added to a green salad and are used to make a tisane or herb tea.
CULTIVATION Hardy annual. Sow seeds in mid-spring in a well-drained, sunny or partly shaded position. Plants will be ready about two months later, and, since only young leaves should be used in cooking, you may wish to sow additional seeds in early summer. Borage leaves are difficult to dry success-fully, but can be frozen.

BURNET, SALAD BURNET
GRANDE PIMPRENELLE

An attractive herb, often found growing wild, with pretty toothed leaves set in pairs along the stem. Used widely in France since the eighteenth century as one of the *fines herbes* that are blanched and chopped for adding to a *ravigote* or *chivry* sauce, or a herb stuffing. Nowadays the young leaves are mainly used in the South of France in a mixed green salad. Burnet is still, occasionally, used to flavour vinegar. Like borage, burnet is said to taste of cucumber.
CULTIVATION Hardy perennial. Grow in a moist soil in sun or partial shade. Water frequently during the growing season. Cut back to encourage fresh leaves.

CHAMOMILE
CAMOMILLE

True chamomile is an annual herb. It is often grown in older herb gardens and the medicinal herb gardens that were attached to a monastery. Chamomile has pretty daisy-like flowers which are dried and sold for making a soothing but slightly bitter-tasting tisane.
CULTIVATION Hardy perennial. Grow in a sunny, well-drained posi-tion. Chamomile flowers from mid-summer to early autumn, during which period the flowers can be harvested and dried.

CAPER
CAPRE

Capers are the pickled buds of a small bush that grows wild in many Mediterranean countries. Large capers are most likely imported from Spain and North Africa, the small aromatic nonpareilles are grown commercially in the Bouches-du-Rhône and the Var regions of France. These are available in jars all over France, and are sold loose, from wooden vats of brine, in local markets of France as a piquant seasoning for sauces like tapenade, marinades, and stuffings for meat, fish and vegetables. The classic French sauces – *gribiche*, *ravigote*, *remoulade* and *tartare* – all include capers.

CARAWAY
CUMIN DES PRÉS

Caraway has attractive feathery leaves very like chervil. They are excellent in salads or, either chopped or in sprigs, used as a garnish for cooked vegetables. However, the herb is mainly grown for its seeds which have a pronounced and dis-tinctive taste. Caraway seeds appear in the cooking of Alsace, especially in dishes of cabbage and potato and in some cakes and biscuits.
CULTIVATION Hardy biennial. A crop of seeds in late summer will be produced from seeds sown in mid-spring, although it is safer to sow the seeds at the beginning of the previous autumn. When the crop is ripe, cut the plants at ground level, and hang them up in small bunches to dry. A piece of paper or a tray placed underneath each bunch will catch falling seeds and so maximize your harvest.

CHERVIL
CERFEUIL

Chervil appears widely in French cooking. The feathery leaves have a delicate aniseed flavour which makes them popular for adding, chopped, as a garnish to soups or cooked vegetables. The young leaves – *pluches* – are delicious in salads. Chervil is one of the herbs, with parsley, chives and tarragon, in the mixture known as *fines herbes* used to flavour an omelette and also as a garnish to grilled steak. Chervil makes excellent herb vinegar.
CULTIVATION Hardy annual. Sow seeds in any soil, in sun or partial shade, between early spring and late summer – you will have leaves for cooking within about two months. You can also grow new plants indoors during the autumn and winter months. Cut away flowering stems to encourage fresh leaf growth and a year-round supply.

CHIVES
CIBOULETTE, CIVETTE, CIVES

The delicate onion-flavour of chives has been widely used in sauces and salads since the seventeenth century. Earlier recipes often interchange chives and spring or Welsh onions,

CHIVES

infections, hence its other name – clear eye. The dull-green, furry leaves have a subtle flavour that just hints at sage. When young and tender the leaves can be cut into ribbons for adding to a green salad. Clary leaves resemble those of borage and, like the latter, they were once popular dipped in batter and fried to make fritters.

CULTIVATION Hardy biennial. Grow in good well-drained soil, in full sun. The leaves are best used fresh, but can be dried or frozen.

CORIANDER

CORIANDRE

As a result of the influence of North Africa, coriander is now more widely grown and used in France. The pretty, parsley-like leaves have a most distinctive and, in my view, delicious taste. The herb is mainly used in dishes that have been brought back to France from its former empire. The small round seed with its spicy, orangey flavour is more widely used, finely ground, as a seasoning in *charcuterie*, or with some vegetables like mushrooms and as a flavouring in cakes.

CULTIVATION Hardy annual. Sow seeds in spring in a sunny position, and water generously to encourage leaf growth from the base. Harvest the seeds in autumn when the seedheads develop a spicy fragrance. Dry on a tray or window-sill, then transfer to an airtight container.

CUMIN

CUMIN

There are some areas of Paris and Marseilles where the delicious, warm smell of ground cumin seed is

almost overpowering. The herb needs a hot climate to grow well and it is usually only seen in a specialist's herb garden. The narrow brown seeds are widely available either whole or ground for using in couscous and other North African dishes. Cumin seed is sometimes used in fancy breads.

CULTIVATION Tender annual. Cumin requires a sunny, sheltered aspect. Sow the seeds in late spring, after the danger of frost has passed. Harvest the seeds when they are fresh – almost as soon as they appear.

DANDELION

PISSENLIT

The bitter-tasting leaves of the dandelion are used as a herb and as a vegetable. In the country, a few leaves of dandelion are blanched in hot water with other herbs to make a green sauce for serving with fish. Although the dandelion grows easily in the wild the leaves are very bitter. Newer varieties with fleshier leaves are grown for the table. About a week before cutting, the plant is covered with an upturned flowerpot to keep out the light. This blanches the leaves, making them paler, less bitter-tasting and more palatable.

Dandelion leaves appear in a salad with hot diced bacon that is popular in many parts of France, and in the mixed green winter salad made in Provence called *mesclun*.

CULTIVATION Hardy perennial. Although it is possible to eat wild dandelion, it is often simpler to grow it from seed. It is best sown in the spring in a sunny position. This makes it easier to blanch the leaves later on, see above.

although the flavour of chives is quite distinctive and superior in most cases. Chives have an affinity with eggs and cream. When finely chopped they make an attractive bright green garnish as an alternative to parsley. They are frequently used as an edging plant in a herb garden. In June and July the mauve flowers are most attractive. These are edible and can be added to salads, either singly or pulled apart into their needle-like blooms.

CULTIVATION Hardy perennial. Chives are easy to grow and increase rapidly. They do well in window-boxes. Grow in fertile, well-drained soil in sun or semi-shade. They die down completely in winter, reappearing the following spring.

CLARY, CLARY-SAGE

TOUTE-BONNE

A rarely grown herb mainly seen in an enthusiast's or a medicinal herb garden. A decoction made from the leaves was once widely used for eye

DILL

ANETH

Although, it is a native of the Mediterranean region, dill does not appear in many dishes in traditional French cookery. The original Larousse had no entry for it. Recently, though, cooks and chefs have started to experiment with the herb especially for curing raw fish, particularly salmon, in the style of gravad lax. Chopped dill goes well in a vinaigrette for potatoes or a green salad. The flower head of this annual herb is used to flavour pickled gherkins or a herb vinegar.

CULTIVATION Hardy annual. For a constant supply of dill throughout the summer and autumn, sow seeds in a sunny position at monthly intervals between early spring and mid-summer. Leaves will be ready for picking about two months later. The seeds can also be harvested.

FENNEL

FENOUIL

This aniseed-flavoured herb grows wild all over Provence and it is used in a bouquet garni for flavouring a *court-bouillon* for fish, and chopped, for adding to a sauce or mayonnaise. The famous *loup de mer grillade au fenouil* uses the dried stalks of the previous year's fennel so that it will burn brightly. Both the green-leaved fennel and an attractive bronze-leaved variety are grown in herb gardens. The dried seeds of the herb are less used, although La Varenne has a recipe for fennel seeds coated in sugar.

CULTIVATION Hardy perennial. Grow in a sunny position and keep well watered. Pick off flowers as

they bloom unless you wish to harvest the seeds. For a winter supply, transfer a few clumps to a greenhouse, or a cool spot indoors.

GARLIC

AIL

Garlic is used all over France but it is in the south, where garlic is grown, that the flavour is particularly characteristic of the cooking. Heads of garlic store well in a cool place, for up to two years, although most people use up their supply in time for the new season. In mid-summer, the freshly harvested green garlic, which has a less pungent flavour, is used to make soups. Peeled cloves of garlic are used in marinades for the famous daubes and ragoûts of Provence and the Languedoc. The herb is essential to *aïoli*, the garlic-rich mayonnaise, and it is used in a great number of both meat and fish dishes of the Midi. Those who like garlic use it liberally. It makes a fine-flavoured vinegar and it is delicious in its own right, cooked slowly and served as a vegetable.

CULTIVATION Bulbous perennial. Plant bulbs in early spring in moist soil and, preferably, a sunny position. Carefully ease plants from the soil in late summer for harvesting. Dry and store in the sun or somewhere very dry indoors.

GERANIUM

PELARGONIUM

For over a century, the rose-scented geranium with its lovely fragrant leaves but scentless flowers has been grown in the Provençal countryside around the town of Grasse for the perfume industry. Rose-geranium

FENNEL

oil is extracted from the leaves and this oil perfumes the food that the leaves are cooked with. Cakes, sugars and ice-creams are all flavoured with the leaves of this plant. Elizabeth David recommends adding two or three leaves to each 500 g (1 lb) of blackberries when making jelly.

This type of geranium is usually grown indoors on a window-sill or in a flower garden.

CULTIVATION Tender perennial. Grow in pots on a window-sill, or grow outside but bring in over winter in all but the warmest climates. Remove flowers to encourage leaf growth.

HORSERADISH

RAIFORT

Although a few small young leaves of this herb are sometimes snipped over a green salad, it is the long, white, tapering root which is valued. The root is scrubbed, peeled and grated before using in a dish.

Horseradish appears in the cooking of north-eastern France where the finely grated root is mixed with thick cream and lemon juice, or with apple purée to make a delicious, peppery sauce for serving with beef and sausages. The strong, pungent taste of horseradish can be used to make a herb vinegar or a herb butter.

CULTIVATION Hardy perennial. Horseradish will grow almost anywhere, but prefers rich soil or partial shade. Small pieces of root planted in spring or autumn will take two years to mature. Harvest roots for cooking in late autumn.

HYSSOP

HYSOPE

This attractive looking herb, with dark-green leaves and deep-blue or pale-pink flowers, has fallen out of fashion in most French cooking. It is still used as a medicinal herb. The leaves have a spicy taste a little like mint but with a bitterness. Hyssop is used in Gascony as one of the herbs in a bouquet garni for flavouring a concentrated purée of tomatoes that is to be preserved for the winter. A sprig of the leaves gives a pleasant flavour to a sugar syrup for fruit. Hyssop looks delightful grown as an edging plant in a herb garden.

CULTIVATION Hardy perennial. Plant at any time between early autumn and mid-spring in well-drained soil in a sunny position. Fresh leaves can be picked throughout the year, but are best before the plant flowers; they can also be dried.

LEMON BALM *A lemon-scented clump of lemon balm grows in the midst of mint, rue, sage and white feverfew.*

JUNIPER

GENIÈVRE

The small, black berries of this prickly-leaved shrub are widely used in the central and eastern areas of France, and in Provence where the bushes grow wild on the hillsides. Juniper berries (*baies de genièvre*) have an aromatic and resinous flavour and are used in marinades and stuffings for game and venison. Robustly flavoured pâtés and terrines often include juniper berries. The berries are pale green in their first year, mid-blue in their second, and blue-black when ready to pick for use.

CULTIVATION Evergreen shrub. Plant in well-drained soil. Juniper prefers to be in full sun but it will tolerate light shade.

LAVENDER

LAVANDE

One of the loveliest sights in Provence is a field of lavender in bloom with the purple flower spikes set above the grey-green foliage. Most of France's lavender goes into the production of oil of lavender which is valuable in the perfume and cosmetic industry.

Lavender-flavoured honey made by bees working the flowers of the herb has been produced in Provence for centuries.

CULTIVATION Hardy evergreen shrub. Grow in a sunny, well-drained position. Flowers for drying should be picked when the blooms are showing but are not fully open. Lavender plants are best replaced every five or six years.

LEMON BALM, MELISSA

CITRONELLE

The leaves of lemon balm are used in salads and to make a calming tisane. They are also used to give a light lemon flavour to milk or cool drinks. In the past, the famous *eau-de-Carmes*, melissa cordial, was produced from lemon balm. The small white flowers are liked by bees which leads to the name melissa, from the Greek for honeybee.

CULTIVATION Hardy perennial. Grow in well-drained soil in full sun, if possible. Cut back in early summer to encourage new growth, and again in early autumn.

KITCHEN GARDEN *When fresh herbs are required in this house near Paris, the cook has only to step outside the door.*

LIME FLOWERS

FLEURS DE TILLEUL

A tisane of lime flowers was once considered to be of immense medicinal value. In nineteenth-century France, the driveway to a hospital was sometimes planted with an avenue of lime trees. The fragrant yellow flowers and bracts appear in early summer when the flowers are picked and dried in a warm, airy place until paper-dry. A delicately scented tisane is made by infusing one teaspoon of flowers in a cup of boiling water. Leave for three minutes then strain. Lime tea is served hot or cold and it also used, warm, for soaking dried fruits.

LOVAGE

LIVÈCHE

An attractive, tall herb with indented leaves which have a delicious flavour. They are used in soups and sometimes included in a bouquet garni with a bay leaf and a slim leek. A few young leaves are added to a green salad and, in some regions, the stalks are eaten like celery. Both the dried seed and the dried root of lovage are used as a flavouring in bread and biscuits.
CULTIVATION Hardy perennial. Grow in good soil in a sunny position. Encourage fresh leaf growth by removing flowers during the summer. The leaves do not dry well, but can be frozen.

MARIGOLD

SOUCI

The young leaves of the annual marigold are added to salads. The orange and yellow petals are sprink-led over salads and, in the past, were used to give colour to butter. They are also used to decorate some cream, milk and sweet dishes. In summer cooking, marigold petals are used fresh; during the rest of the year dried petals are usually available on market herb stalls.
CULTIVATION Half-hardy annual. Grow in a sunny position, in any soil, from seed. Marigolds self-seed freely but tend to legginess in the shade. The flowers appear from late spring onwards.

MARJORAM

MARJOLAINE

The botanical name for all marjorams is *origanum*. Sweet, or knotted, marjoram is the annual herb whose leaves are much favoured for

MINT

flavouring meat and some *charcuterie*. Pot marjoram is a perennial herb with less fragrant leaves, and wild marjoram, which is also known as oregano, grows freely in Provence and is widely used in the cooking of southern France.

Marjoram is an excellent herb for using fresh or dried. It goes well with many meats and is used in sausages and terrines.
CULTIVATION Annual and perennial. Grow in well-drained soil in a sunny position. Trim back if the plant spreads and cut back hard once or twice a year to encourage fresh leaf growth. Pick leaves for drying or freezing before the flowers open in mid-summer.

MINT

MENTHE

Although still used far less in French cooking than in British, mint is a herb that is gradually gaining favour. It appears in the classic *sauce paloise* which is béarnaise sauce flavoured with mint and served with lamb. Young mint leaves are occasionally added to a mixed green salad, to other vegetables and to some sweet dishes in the form of Crème de Menthe liqueur. Mint tea is a popular digestive taken in place of coffee at the end of a late meal.
CULTIVATION Hardy perennial, Mint prefers rich soil and light shade. It requires little care other than removing flowers and checking that it does not become too invasive – it is sometimes best to grow it in a pot, or in a bucket sunk in the ground. To provide a supply of fresh mint during the winter, place a few plants in pots and stand them indoors on a window-sill.

NASTURTIUM

CAPUCINE

This annual is grown as a garden flower and as a herb. In the South of France, nasturtiums are often sown at the foot of a garden fig tree. Both the leaves and the flowers are eaten and the green seeds are sometimes pickled to produce a kind of substitute caper. The leaves can be stuffed and cooked like vine leaves while the flowers are used to decorate a salad. Nasturtium flowers make a fine, peppery-flavoured vinegar that also takes on the colour of the flowers.

CULTIVATION Hardy annual. Nasturtiums grow easily from seed, and self-seed well. Plant in a sunny position, in rich soil. This encourages leafy growth, or if you wish, poorer soil will produce more flowers.

OREGANO

ORIGAN

This is the wild form of marjoram. Used fresh or dried, it appears in some of the Italian-inspired dishes of Nice and the surrounding area. Oregano goes particularly well with tomatoes, cooked cheese dishes and strongly flavoured meats. The variegated form makes an attractive hummock shape in the herb garden. See also Marjoram.

PARSLEY

PERSIL

This is an important herb in French cookery. Both the curly form (*frisé*) and the far more aromatic flat-leaf (*commun* or *d'Italie*) variety are used in many dishes. A sprig of parsley is part of the classic bouquet garni and

the herb also appears in *fines herbes*. Indeed, no other herb appears alongside another as often as parsley. Its delightful flavour is as concentrated in the stalks as in the leaves. A cream sauce flavoured solely with parsley has a freshness no other herb can match. As with most herbs it is particularly important to chop parsley at the last moment so that the full flavour of the aromatic oils is captured in the dish.

Whole leaves of flat parsley make an appealing garnish, rather more so than the over-used chopped parsley. Finely chopped parsley is, however, essential for making a *persillade* which is a mixture of parsley, finely chopped shallot and grated zest of lemon. A *persillade* is added to a dish, especially a dish of fish or veal, in the final stages of cooking.

OREGANO

CULTIVATION Hardy biennial. Sow seeds outdoors in spring in a sunny position. Parsley is a cut-and-come-again herb, so not many plants will be needed. It is difficult to dry successfully, although it can be frozen. The best way to ensure a year-round supply is to transfer a couple of plants indoors in autumn to last through the winter.

PURSLANE

POURPIER

A fleshy leaved herb with mid-green or yellow-green leaves that grows wild in some parts of Provence. The delicious, slightly nutty-tasting, purslane leaves are used raw in salads or when cooked, are served as an alternative to spinach. Purslane was once very popular in the South of France; there are nineteenth-century recipes for a purslane gratin and a purslane sauce. Recently this herb has started to return to favour. Both green and golden purslane are quick and easy to grow.

CULTIVATION Hardy annual. Sow seeds in spring in a moist, semi-shaded position. Leaves will be ready for picking within six weeks. Water occasionally if the plant is beginning to wilt.

ROCAMBOLE

ROCAMBOLE

Depending on the season and the time of planting, this mild-tasting type of garlic forms a bulb that divides into cloves or grows into a single bulb like an onion. Rocambole can also develop small immature bulbils in the stem a few inches above the ground. Once widely grown in the South of

France, nineteenth-century recipes often refer to the herb, however, it is now rarely seen except in specialist herb gardens. Rocambole is a herb worth reviving which can be used in place of onions. See also Garlic.

ROCKET

ROQUETTE

Leafy green rocket has a distinctive taste rather like peanuts. It is added to mixed green salads, and just a few leaves improve the flavour of most lettuces. The herb is included in the Provençal mixture of leaves known as *mesclun*, and the white flowers can be used to decorate a salad.
CULTIVATION Hardy annual. Ensure a continuous supply of leaves by sowing seeds at regular intervals from early spring to early summer in well-watered soil. Pick off flowering stems to encourage leaf growth.

ROSEMARY

ROMARIN

The grey-green needle-shaped leaves of this delightful evergreen shrub carry pale-blue – and in some varieties, pink or white – flowers in early summer and at intervals during the rest of the year. Rosemary leaves are used for seasoning grilled and roast meat, especially lamb and veal. Young branches of the herb are used as skewers for meat, fish or vegetable kebabs especially in outdoor cooking. Rosemary grows wild in the South of France and it is one of the constituents of *herbes de Provence*. The fresh herb is more subtle in flavour than the dried form.
CULTIVATION Hardy evergreen shrub. Grow in well-drained soil in a sunny position.

SUMMER SAVORY *Both summer and winter savory taste slightly of thyme, but winter savory is more peppery.*

SAGE

SAUGE

This evergreen herb with grey velvety leaves grows wild in Mediterranean regions. Its distinctive flavour is used with pork and veal and in seasoning some *charcuterie*. Both the leaves and the deep-blue flowers are used to flavour an *eau-de-vie* in northern Provence. The flowers are used to decorate salads. There are several varieties of sage, with red, variegated and tricolour leaves, but the grey-leaved variety has the most pronounced flavour. Sage is best used sparingly and the fresh leaves are preferable to the dried which can develop a musty flavour after a while.
CULTIVATION Hardy evergreen shrub. Grow in a sunny, well-drained spot. Trim regularly, and replace every three or four years.

SAVORY

SARRIETTE

There are two main forms of this herb: the white-flowered summer savory which is an annual, and the perennial winter variety with its pale-lavender flowers. A wild savory, known as *poivre d'âne*, grows in Provence. The herb has a slightly bitter taste that is similar to thyme. Summer savory is traditionally grown alongside, and is served with, broad beans. Winter savory has a peppery, coarser flavour; it is sometimes included in a bouquet garni for meat stews.
CULTIVATION Hardy annual and perennial. Grow both summer and winter savory in a sunny well-drained position. Replace winter savory every two or three years.

SORREL

OSEILLE

The cultivated form of sorrel is widely used all over France. The fresh leaves are bright green and crisp, although like spinach they flag quickly. The young leaves are used in salads and their sharp, lemony flavour perks up many a green salad. When cooked, the leaves shrink dramatically and turn into a dull olive-green purée which goes admirably with rich food and is the basis for many sauces, especially those for serving with fish and eggs, and for a classic sorrel soup. A few leaves of sorrel are often included when cooking spinach.
CULTIVATION Hardy perennial. Grow in rich moist soil in sun or semi-shade. Sorrel self-seeds readily. Remove any flower stalks as they appear to encourage leaf growth.

SWEET CICELY

CERFEUIL D'ESPAGNE

The downy, lacy leaves of this tall herb taste slightly of aniseed and liquorice. Like angelica, sweet cicely has a sweetening effect on acid fruit. The young leaves make a decorative addition to a green salad or a salad of wild leaves. Sweet cicely is a pretty member of the Umbelliferae family and is worth a place towards the back of a herb bed.

CULTIVATION Perennial. Grow in a shady moist position.

TARRAGON

ESTRAGON

It is unfortunate for the cook that there are two tarragons. Russian tarragon is not worth growing as a culinary herb. Its coarse, undeveloped flavour will only disappoint, whereas the French tarragon, with its deliciously refreshing aniseed-like flavour, is one of the essential herbs in a civilized kitchen.

Tarragon is a summer herb and it goes well with much summer food. It is one of the constituents of *fines herbes*. In France, its uncannily successful alliance with chicken is well known. The herb also flatters many lightly cooked vegetables, especially in a tarragon butter used as a simple sauce just before serving. Fresh tarragon makes one of the most delightful herb-flavoured vinegars for salads.

CULTIVATION Hardy perennial. Grow in a well-drained, sunny position. Protect the plants from frost and damp, if possible, during winter. The soft stem dies down in winter, and tarragon very seldom produces any flowers.

VERVAIN *The leaves of vervain are used to flavour a liqueur as well as being the basis of a tonic infusion.*

THYME

THYM

This strongly aromatic herb is one of the most successful for drying. In France, the dried leaves are also pulverized and sold as thyme powder which can be useful for seasoning a fine-texture mixture or a sauce. On the whole, though, I prefer fresh herbs for cooking, and some varieties of thyme, for example lemon thyme – *thym de citron* – lose most of their charm when dried. A sprig of thyme is part of the classic bouquet garni. Thyme is a powerful herb and should be used with discretion. French cooks add it to a wide variety of meat dishes. It is used lavishly in Provençal cooking, and all over France thyme is one of the major herbs used in *charcuterie*.

Wild-thyme – *serpolet* – grows freely all over the Midi. In Provence it is known as *farigoule* and *frigolet*.

CULTIVATION Hardy evergreen shrub. Grow in well-drained soil in a warm, sheltered position. In cold climates, bring plants inside during winter. Thyme leaves are most aromatic when young.

VERBENA AND VERVAIN

VERVEINE ODORANTE ET VERVEINE OFFICINALE

Lemon-scented verbena (*Lippia citriodora*) is grown in France for its fragrant oil which is used in the cosmetic industry. The leaves of this herb make a cooling tisane and they are also used to flavour sugars and sweet dishes. When used in conjunction with fresh lemon, the flavour is akin to fresh lime. Verbena is well worth growing in the herb garden simply for the scent it releases when you brush your hands over the leaves on a still evening.

Although a member of the same family, vervain (*Verbena officinalis*) has a restricted use in the kitchen; it is more commonly employed medicinally. However, in the centre of Le Puy there is a large neon sign advertising *Verveine du Velay*, a famous vervain-flavoured liqueur that is made in the region. I always wonder whether the success of this drink has any connection with a vervain tisane which has an ancient reputation as a love potion.

CULTIVATION Tender shrub and hardy perennial. Grow lemon verbena in well-drained soil in full sun with shelter. Protect during the winter in cooler climates. Grow vervain in a sunny, well-drained position. Although perennial, vervain is at its best in its first year.

Les Hors-D'œuvres —et— Les Soupes

FIRST
COURSES AND
SOUPS

*Soup is the most traditional overture
to a meal in France and the variety
of French soups is astonishing,
but there is many
another appetizing first course
to choose from.*

PISSALADIÈRE *left (p. 42)*, AUBERGINES AUX
ANCHOIS *right (p. 35)*.

First, I look for the right signs. A row of table napkins on a washing line, blowing in the breeze, sparkling windows and pretty flowers – even if growing in an old painted can – are hopeful. And then, if the place is comfortably busy with local people, I look at the menu. Reading the *prix fixe* menu of seasonal dishes I decide that things look promising.

In France, I like to eat in small, country restaurants and only rarely have I been disappointed. Their style of cooking – often described by the patron as *cuisine soigneuse*, careful cooking, is skilled and discriminating, and it presents the classic food of rural France in a fresh and satisfying way. Always delicious, it is often superb.

For me, the excitement of eating in France never palls. Sitting down at an immaculate table (even a small café or bar provides a sparkling white paper cover), I immediately have to touch it, as a kind of talisman, to feel reassured. I sit back, spread the napkin over my lap and allow myself to feel hungry.

A basket of bread is placed on the table – a baguette cut in pieces, each light, lacy slice creamy-white and encased in a golden crust. I start to eat it, spreading small pieces with the sweet unsalted butter of northern France and I anticipate the start of another good French meal.

Soup arrives in a splendid tureen. My favourite places leave the tureen on the table for you to help yourself to more. I remember a big, white porcelain bowl of pale green soup with tiny flecks of darker green. It pours like thin cream, it tastes of leeks and potatoes and chervil, and it is so smooth and buttery you can't stop eating it.

Although there is many another appetizing first course to a French meal, soup is the most traditional. And so important is the dish that, in the country, the evening meal – *le souper* – is named after it.

The variety and range of French soups is astonishing. Many of the best are very simple – little more than a purée of one or two vegetables thinned with stock or cream and seasoned with herbs. The freshness of the ingredients and the subtlety of their seasoning is what gives them distinction. Such a soup is finished with a little butter, or best of all, a herb butter which gives the soup an unforgettably good aroma and taste. Little compares with a bowl of richly smooth tomato soup with a thin disc of tarragon butter melting on top.

HERB BUTTERS

In the summer, one of the most enjoyable kitchen tasks is making a range of herb butters. The process is simple enough. This basic recipe is for *maître d'hôtel* butter which can then be varied.

Cream 115 g (4 oz) of unsalted butter, then gradually beat in 1 tablespoon of lemon juice and 2 tablespoons of finely chopped parsley. Season to taste with salt and freshly milled pepper. *Maître d'hôtel* butter goes well with grilled fish, steak and hot vegetables.

For speed I sometimes use a food processor but I really prefer to take time over this pleasurable task. For a very smooth result pass the flavoured butter through a fine sieve before storing it, but on the whole I prefer the speckled look of the unsieved butter.

To store herb butters, spoon the flavoured butter on to a double thickness of greaseproof paper and shape into a long roll. Chill until firm, then cut into thin slices. Wrap, label and store in a refrigerator for up to 2 weeks or in a freezer for up to 3 months.

GARLIC BUTTER Add 1 or 2 crushed cloves of garlic to the basic recipe. Garlic butter is delicious on grilled steak, or hot potatoes and warm bread.

CHIVE BUTTER Make as for *maître d'hôtel* butter but add finely chopped chives instead of parsley. Chive butter is excellent with eggs, steamed carrots or cauliflower.

TARRAGON BUTTER Blanch 1–2 tablespoons tarragon leaves, drain and refresh under cold water. Small, tender leaves can be used raw. Chop very finely and use instead of parsley in the basic recipe. Use tarragon butter with grilled chicken or fish, and light summer soups.

RAVIGOTE BUTTER Blanch 1 finely chopped shallot and 2–3 tablespoons mixed parsley, chervil, tarragon and chive leaves. Refresh in cold water then drain well and chop. Add to the softened butter in the basic recipe in place of parsley. Sieve for a really smooth butter.

CRÈME DE CHAMPIGNONS AU CERFEUIL SOUS CROÛTE

CREAM OF MUSHROOM SOUP UNDER A CRUST

Breaking through the pastry crust that covers this soup releases the wonderful aroma of buttery mushrooms and chervil. Ideally, make this soup in individual dishes so that each person can savour the fragrance, but it can be presented in one large ovenproof tureen covered with a lid of light, golden pastry. The soup can also be served without the pastry crust.

SERVES 4 – 6

340 g (12 oz) mushrooms
85 g (3 oz) butter
1 small onion, finely chopped
1 clove garlic, finely chopped
1 tablespoon lemon juice
500 ml (generous $\frac{3}{4}$ pint) chicken stock
150 ml ($\frac{1}{4}$ pint) milk
1 tablespoon flour or potato flour
150 ml ($\frac{1}{4}$ pint) double cream
1 tablespoon chopped chervil
2 teaspoons finely chopped parsley
1 tablespoon Manzanilla sherry
salt and freshly milled pepper
180 g (6 oz) prepared-weight puff pastry
1 egg, separated
a few leaves of chervil for decoration

Wipe the mushrooms with a damp cloth, remove a thin layer from the end of each stalk and discard. Slice the mushrooms thinly. Melt half the butter in a pan and sauté 1 tablespoon of the mushrooms until soft. Use a slotted spoon to transfer the mushrooms to a plate and set aside for the garnish.

Add the remaining butter to the pan and cook the onion and garlic until soft. Stir in the mushrooms until they have absorbed the butter and add the lemon juice.

Pour in the stock, cover the pan and cook over moderate heat for 15 minutes.

Purée the contents of the pan in a food processor or liquidizer and return to the pan. Blend the milk with the flour and stir into the soup. Cook, stirring, until thickened.

Add the cream, chervil, parsley, sherry, and salt and pepper to taste. Pour the soup into individual ovenproof bowls or one large dish, making sure that the dishes are only three-quarters full.

Roll out the pastry and cut a lid for each of the dishes. Brush the rim of each dish with egg white and cover with a pastry lid, pressing the edges down well. Crimp the edge of the pastry, brush with egg yolk and cut 2 or 3 vents in the centre to allow steam to escape.

Place the soup dishes on a baking sheet and bake in a hot oven (200°C, 400°F, gas mark 7) for 15 – 20 minutes until the pastry is golden brown and well puffed up. Wrap the reserved slices of mushroom in foil and reheat in the oven.

To serve, garnish each pastry lid with 2 or 3 slices of mushroom and decorate with a sprig of chervil. If the soup has been cooked in one large dish, ladle it into soup bowls and float a wedge of pastry in each just before serving.

SOUPE DE TOMATE À L'ESTRAGON

TOMATO AND TARRAGON SOUP

Fresh tarragon brings out the delightful summer taste of ripe tomatoes in this simple soup. I like to serve it hot on a summer evening as a preface to a cold main course.

SERVES 4

55 g (2 oz) butter
1 small onion, chopped
$\frac{1}{2}$ clove garlic, finely chopped
$\frac{1}{2}$ stick celery, chopped
680 g ($1\frac{1}{2}$ lb) ripe tomatoes, peeled and chopped
150 ml ($\frac{1}{4}$ pint) dry white wine
1 bay leaf
4 allspice berries
a strip of orange peel
1 teaspoon sugar
salt
1 tablespoon fresh tarragon leaves, chopped
GARNISH
150 ml ($\frac{1}{4}$ pint) crème fraîche (optional)
a few extra tarragon leaves

Melt half the butter in a pan and stir in the onion, garlic and celery. Cook gently for 3 minutes. Add the tomatoes, wine, bay leaf, allspice, orange peel, sugar, a little salt and half the tarragon. Bring to the boil, cover and cook for 25–30 minutes.

Press the contents of the pan through a fine sieve and check the seasoning. Add the remaining tarragon, bring back almost to the boil and add the remaining butter. Serve, garnished with *crème fraîche* or tarragon.

SOUPE DE TOMATE À L'ESTRAGON *left*, CRÈME DE CHAMPIGNONS AU CERFEUIL *centre (p. 27)*, SOUPE AU PISTOU *right (p. 30)*.

SOUPE AU PISTOU

BEAN AND VEGETABLE SOUP WITH PISTOU

This is a beautiful, classic soup from the Mediterranean area of Provence. Fresh white haricot beans are available in France in late July and August. During the rest of the year, dried beans are used. Pistou sauce, made with fresh basil, garlic and olive oil, makes a fine last-minute addition to many summer vegetable soups.

SERVES 6

1 tablespoon olive oil

1 medium onion, finely chopped

115 g (4 oz) fresh white haricot beans, or soaked and cooked dried haricot beans

2 medium potatoes, diced

1 stick celery, chopped

salt and freshly milled pepper

225 g (8 oz) French beans, cut in short lengths

the green part of a leek, finely sliced

2 tomatoes, peeled and chopped

55 g (2 oz) fine vermicelli

PISTOU

2–3 cloves garlic

a handful of basil leaves

3–4 tablespoons olive oil

freshly grated Parmesan or Gruyère cheese

Heat the oil in a large pan and soften the onion. Add the white haricot beans, potatoes and celery with about 1.5 litres (2½–3 pints) of water and some salt and pepper. Simmer, covered, for 10–15 minutes.

Add the French beans, the leek, tomatoes and vermicelli and cook for a further 10 minutes.

Meanwhile pound the peeled cloves of garlic in a mortar or chop finely in a processor with the basil, gradually adding the olive oil and just a tablespoon or so of the hot liquid from the soup.

Serve the soup in large bowls, spoon in some pistou and sprinkle the cheese on top.

SOUPE DE POISSONS AVEC LA ROUILLE

FISH SOUP WITH ROUILLE SAUCE

All over the Midi this rust-red soup is served in small bars and restaurants. Traditionally the soup is accompanied by *croûtons* of toasted French bread, Gruyère cheese and a bowl of the fiery tasting and garlic-rich *rouille* sauce.

SERVES 4

SOUP

2–3 tablespoons olive oil

1 medium onion, chopped

1–2 cloves garlic, chopped

680 g (1½ lb) fish, ideally small fish sold specially for soup

225 g (8 oz) tomatoes, peeled and chopped

1 bouquet garni

1 litre (1¾ pints) water

150 ml (¼ pint) red wine

salt and a few peppercorns

½ teaspoon saffron strands

ROUILLE

1 red chilli pepper, fresh or dried

2–3 cloves garlic

85 g (3 oz) white bread, without crusts

6–8 tablespoons olive oil

1 teaspoon tomato purée

TO SERVE

half a baguette or French stick

Gruyère cheese, finely grated

Heat the oil in a large saucepan, stir in the onion and garlic and cook until soft but do not allow to colour. Add the fish and turn it over in the oil. Add the tomatoes, bouquet garni, water, wine, salt and peppercorns and bring to the boil. Cover the pan, turn down the heat and gently simmer the soup for 30–40 minutes.

Strain the soup through a sieve, lightly pressing the fish to extract the full flavour. Return the liquid to the pan, add the saffron and simmer for 20 minutes to take the colour and flavour from the spice. Taste and adjust the flavouring of the soup.

To make the *rouille*, halve and seed the red chilli pepper (if using a dried pepper soak it in warm water for a few minutes to soften) and chop finely. Pound the chilli pepper to a paste in a mortar with the garlic. Soak the bread in cold water, squeeze dry and gradually work into the chilli paste with the olive oil, beating well all the time as for mayonnaise. Blend in the tomato purée and spoon the sauce into a pottery bowl.

Slice and toast the bread to make *croûtons*. Serve the soup in hot bowls and hand round the *rouille*, toasted *croûtons* and grated cheese separately. Each person floats a *croûton* or two – covered with *rouille* or cheese or both – on top of the soup, stirring to incorporate all the flavours.

TRIMMING GARLIC *Bundles of garlic heads are hung up to dry in rows, high in a dark airy barn in Gers. The heads are then plaited into chains or simply trimmed and put into sacks before being sent to the market to be sold.*

SOUPE AUX CHÂTAIGNES ET AUX OIGNONS

CHESTNUT AND ONION SOUP

The beautiful Ardèche region of France is the home of the sweet chestnut, and its main town, Privas, is the capital of the world's *marron glacé* production. In this remote and mountainous area, the chestnut has always played a major part in domestic life. Chestnut trees were once known as bread trees because even the bread was made with chestnut flour. This warming chestnut soup is a good restorative on a cold winter evening.

SERVES 4 – 5

225 g (8 oz) chestnuts
3 sprigs of thyme or serpolet (wild thyme)
salt
750 ml (1¼ pints) chicken or vegetable stock
2 medium onions, chopped
1 tablespoon olive oil
bouquet garni
freshly milled pepper

TO SERVE
a splash of milk or cream
croûtons *fried in oil*

Peel the outer skin from the chestnuts. Place the chestnuts in a pan and cover with cold water. Add one of the sprigs of thyme and some salt and bring to the boil. Simmer for 20 minutes or until the chestnuts are tender. Pour off the cooking liquid and, when the chestnuts are cool enough to handle, rub off the thin papery inner skins. Purée the chestnuts with some of the stock using a food processor or a mouli-legumes.

Soften the onions in the oil and cook until golden but not brown. Add the remaining stock and thyme, and the bouquet garni. Bring to the boil. Simmer for 10 minutes then add the chestnut purée and cook for a further 5 minutes. Check the flavour and season with salt and pepper.

Just before serving remove the herbs and add the milk or cream. Serve the soup with hot *croûtons*.

POTAGE GLACÉ À L'OSEILLE

ICED SORREL SOUP

Traditionally in France, sorrel was eaten in the spring, before Easter, as a tonic and purifier after the unhealthy winter months. This is a beautiful springtime soup made pleasantly astringent by the lemon-flavoured herb.

SERVES 4 — 5

115 g (4 oz) sorrel leaves
1 large cucumber, peeled and chopped
1 clove garlic
1 litre (1¾ pints) light chicken stock or water
150 ml (¼ pint) double cream
salt
a dash of Tabasco sauce
a little finely chopped chervil or parsley

A LAWN OF THYME *A glorious swathe of purple thyme adorns a garden in the Côte d'Azur. It is a garden variety of the serpolet that grows wild on the Provence hillsides.*

Wash and drain the sorrel and chop roughly. Place in a pan with the cucumber, the clove of garlic and stock or water. Bring to the boil then cook steadily over moderate heat until the cucumber is soft.

Remove from the heat and pass through a mouli-legumes on its finest setting or reduce to a smooth purée in a food processor or liquidizer. Chill the soup then whisk in the cream and season to taste with salt and a little Tabasco sauce.

Serve in a tureen with a little finely chopped chervil sprinkled on top.

SOUPE AU MELON ET AUX NECTARINES

MELON AND NECTARINE SOUP

Fruit soups are very cooling served lightly chilled on a hot day. Freshly chopped mint emphasizes the delicately scented flavour of the melon and nectarines.

SERVES 4 — 6

1 ripe Galia or cantaloup melon
3 — 4 ripe nectarines
juice of 1 orange
sugar to taste
salt
1 — 2 drops Tabasco sauce
a dash of balsamic or sherry vinegar
1 tablespoon finely chopped mint
a few extra sprigs of mint for decoration

Halve the melon and discard the seeds. Scoop the flesh into a food processor or liquidizer. Wash and dry the nectarines and slice the fruit into the processor. Add the juice of an orange and process until puréed. Season to taste with sugar, salt and Tabasco sauce, then add the vinegar and chopped mint. Chill the soup for 30 minutes.

Serve in chilled dishes or glasses and decorate with sprigs of mint.

PÂTÉ DE GIBIER AU GENIÈVRE

GAME PÂTÉ WITH JUNIPER BERRIES

This pâté, which is actually more like a potted meat, is quick to make because the game is already cooked. In fact, this is a delicious way of making the most of any meat left on a carcass after carving. Pheasant, partridge, hare, wild duck, rabbit, pigeon and venison are all suitable for this recipe.

SERVES 3 – 4

225 g (8 oz) cooked game, boned
85 g (3 oz) butter
1 shallot, chopped
1 slim clove garlic, chopped
4 juniper berries, crushed
150 ml ($\frac{1}{4}$ pint) double cream
1 tablespoon brandy
salt and freshly milled pepper

Cut the meat into even-sized pieces, then chop roughly in a food processor.

Melt half the butter in a pan and cook the shallot and garlic until soft but not coloured. Add the juniper berries and stir over the heat to extract the flavour. Allow to cool slightly then add to the meat in the processor, with the remaining butter. Purée until fairly smooth.

Whisk the cream with the brandy until stiff. Fold into the meat mixture and season to taste with salt and pepper. Spoon the mixture into a pot or dish and smooth level. Chill for 24 hours before serving with hot toast or rolls.

BASIL FOR SALE *Pots of basil on a market stall are labelled 'Pistou' to remind customers that basil is the main ingredient of pistou sauce made with olive oil, garlic and cheese. Basil is one of the characteristic flavours of the cooking of Provence. It is much less used in northern France. A variety with medium-sized leaves is most common.*

TARTELETTES AUX CHAMPIGNONS

MUSHROOM AND BASIL TARTLETS

When I am in France, I cook wild mushrooms, especially *cèpes*, in this way. If there is no time to search meadows and woodlands you can often find wild mushrooms being sold on a market stall, collected by the stall-holder first thing that morning. In this country, where we are less familiar with wild fungi, small cultivated mushrooms make a delicious filling.

SERVES 6

PÂTE BRISÉE
115 g (4 oz) plain flour
55 g (2 oz) butter
1 egg yolk
1 – 2 tablespoons cold water
a pinch of salt

FILLING

180 g (6 oz) button or small cap mushrooms
45 g (1½ oz) butter
2 spring onions, chopped
1 tablespoon plain flour
150 ml (¼ pint) single cream
salt and freshly milled pepper
1 tablespoon chopped fresh basil
a few leaves of flat-leaf parsley

Sieve the flour into a heap on a cold work surface or into a wide chilled bowl. Make a well in the centre and add the butter, egg yolk and water mixed with the pinch of salt.

Work the ingredients together with your fingertips, gradually drawing the flour into the centre until the mixture forms small lumps. Take these and push them away from you on the work surface, using the heel of your hand to spread the dough, then scrape it together with the blade of a knife or a pastry scraper until the dough forms a ball. Wrap the pastry and chill for 30 minutes.

Meanwhile, make the filling. Wipe the mushrooms with a damp cloth and leave whole if they are very small, otherwise quarter them. Melt the butter in a pan and cook the mushrooms with the spring onions until they are soft. Lift out with a slotted spoon and set aside until the pastry cases are ready to be filled.

Roll out the pastry to line six 10 cm (4 in) tartlet tins. Prick the pastry bases and bake on a preheated baking sheet in a hot oven (200°C, 400°F, gas mark 6), for about 10 minutes until the pastry is set but has not started to colour.

Stir the flour into the pan and cook over moderate heat for 1–2 minutes. Gradually add the cream and cook gently until the mixture has thickened. Season with salt and pepper and stir in the basil. Divide the mushrooms between the tart cases and spoon the sauce over. Reheat the tarts in the oven for 5–7 minutes until the sauce bubbles.

Decorate each tart with a parsley leaf and serve straight away.

AUBERGINES AUX ANCHOIS

AUBERGINES WITH ANCHOVIES

In this simple Provençal dish the glossy, purple-skinned aubergine is halved and stuffed with an aromatic mixture of herbs and anchovies. The surprisingly subtle, slightly smoky flavour of the dish is most delicious when the aubergines are served cold.

SERVES 4

2–4 aubergines (depending on size)
1 shallot, finely chopped
1 clove garlic, chopped
4 anchovy fillets
1 tablespoon fresh basil
1 tablespoon fresh parsley
3–4 tablespoons olive oil
2–3 large ripe tomatoes, sliced

Wipe the aubergines and halve them lengthwise. Place them cut side down on the work surface and make three or four lengthwise cuts, but not all the way through, to resemble the leaves of a book.

Pound the shallot, garlic, anchovies, basil and parsley with a little olive oil in a pestle and mortar, or chop the ingredients together in a food processor, to make a paste.

Spread the anchovy paste over all the cut surfaces of the aubergines and insert slices of tomato in the cuts. Arrange the stuffed aubergines in an oiled ovenproof dish and trickle the remaining oil over the top. Add 2 tablespoons of warm water to the dish and cover.

Cook in a moderate oven (180°C, 350°F, gas mark 4) for 30–45 minutes or until the aubergines are cooked. Set aside to cool and serve warm or cold with hot, crusty bread.

BEIGNETS DES FLEURS DE COURGETTE

COURGETTE-FLOWER FRITTERS

Sometimes in country markets in the South of France you will see a heap of courgette flowers for sale. The deep-yellow blossoms are soon snapped up and taken home before they wilt in the heat. In Provence the flowers are dipped into a light batter and deep-fried to make a delightful appetizer that is served before the noonday meal. If you grow courgettes, pick the large (male) flowers in the morning, soon after the flowers have opened and the dew has dried.

MAKES 20–24

20–24 courgette flowers
100 g (3$\frac{1}{2}$ oz) plain flour
a pinch of salt
1 tablespoon olive oil
1 egg, separated
about 150 ml ($\frac{1}{4}$ pint) warm water
mild-flavoured oil, such as sunflower, for deep-frying
salt and herbes de Provence for serving

Remove the stalks from the courgette flowers. If the flowers are at all dusty, wash them gently in cold water and drain well.

Sieve the flour and salt into a bowl and mix in the oil, egg yolk and enough water to make a batter that resembles pouring cream. Whisk the egg white until stiff and fold into the batter.

Heat the oil to frying temperature, 180°C (355°F). Dip a flower into the batter to coat it and then lower it into the hot oil and cook until golden. Lift out and drain on kitchen paper. Cook the rest of the flowers in the same way. Serve straight away, sprinkled with salt and *herbes de Provence*.

Any batter left over can be used to make crêpes, or pancakes.

SORBET DE MENTHE AU MELON

PINEAPPLE-MINT SORBET WITH MELON

Pineapple mint or a well-flavoured spearmint give this sorbet the best flavour. I like to serve the sorbet on a slice of chilled melon resting on a vine leaf and decorated with a sprig of crystallized mint leaves.

SERVES 4–6

225 g (8 oz) granulated sugar
425 ml ($\frac{3}{4}$ pint) water
1 lemon
a large handful of mint leaves
green food colouring (optional)
CRYSTALLIZED MINT LEAVES
4–6 sprigs of mint
2 egg whites
1 tablespoon caster sugar
TO SERVE
1 ripe green-fleshed melon, preferably Galia
4–6 vine leaves

Make the crystallized mint leaves first so that they have plenty of time to dry. Cut the stalks from the sprigs of mint or use about 12 separate mint leaves instead. Lightly whisk the egg whites and brush the leaves on both sides. (Reserve the remaining egg white.) Sprinkle with caster sugar, lay on grease-proof paper and leave in a warm place to dry.

To make the sorbet, dissolve the sugar in the water, add a strip of lemon peel and bring to the boil. Simmer for 5 minutes then take the syrup off the heat and cool for a minute or two.

Chop the mint leaves roughly and place in a bowl with the juice of the lemon. Pour the hot, but not boiling, syrup over the leaves. Set aside until cold. Strain the syrup into a bowl and add just 1 drop of green food colouring to make the sorbet

pale green. Freeze for about 2 hours until mushy.

Whisk the egg whites until stiff, fold into the half-frozen syrup and refreeze.

To serve, lay a vine leaf on each plate and place a slice of melon on top. Beat the sorbet until soft and spoon some into the centre of the melon. Decorate with the crystallized mint leaves and serve.

MIST AND DEW *Watery sunshine glimmers through early morning mist on to dew-sprinkled mint, hyssop, fennel and other herbs. All are in a final burst of flower as summer changes to autumn and the overgrown leaves tumble on to the brick paths softening the formal lines of the garden.*

37

TARTELETTES AUX TOMATES

TOMATO TARTLETS

These small savoury tarts are the speciality of a baker in Privas in the Ardèche. The crisp pastry contrasts well with the aromatic filling of the tomatoes flavoured with thyme or serpolet (wild thyme), bay and marjoram, garnished with anchovies and olives.

SERVES 6

PÂTE BRISÉE
115 g (4 oz) plain flour
55 g (2 oz) butter, at room temperature
1 egg yolk
2 tablespoons iced water
a pinch of salt

FILLING
1 medium onion, chopped
1 clove garlic, finely chopped
1 tablespoon olive oil
450 g (1 lb) tomatoes, peeled and chopped
½ teaspoon caster sugar
a sprig of thyme or serpolet
1 bay leaf
salt and freshly milled pepper
1 teaspoon finely chopped marjoram
about 12 anchovy fillets or black olives

Sieve the flour into a heap on a cold work surface or into a wide, chilled bowl. Make a well in the centre and add the butter, egg yolk and water mixed with the pinch of salt.

Work the ingredients together with your fingertips, gradually drawing the flour into the centre until the mixture forms small lumps. Take these and push them away from you on the work surface, using the heel of your hand to spread the dough. Then scrape it together with the blade of a knife or a pastry scraper until the dough forms a ball. Wrap the pastry and chill for 30 minutes.

Meanwhile make the filling. Cook the onion and garlic in the oil for 5 minutes until soft. Add the tomatoes, sugar, thyme and bay leaf. Season lightly with salt and pepper and cook the mixture, uncovered, for 25–30 minutes until almost all the liquid has evaporated. Remove the herbs and purée the mixture in a processor or push through a sieve. Mix in the chopped marjoram.

Roll out the pastry and line six lightly buttered 10 cm (4 in) tartlet tins with it. Prick the pastry bases and chill for 15 minutes. Bake in a hot oven (200°C, 400°F, gas mark 6) for 10–15 minutes until lightly coloured.

Spoon the filling into the pastry cases. Decorate the tartlets with a criss-cross of anchovy fillets and some black olives. Reheat in the oven for 10 minutes until piping hot, taking care that the pastry does not burn. Serve hot, warm or cold.

OEUFS À LA MAYONNAISE À L'ESTRAGON

EGGS IN TARRAGON MAYONNAISE

Mayonnaise is one of the great foods of the world. At one level it is a simple and luxurious sauce that flatters every food it accompanies, even hard-boiled eggs. Yet this remarkable liaison of eggs and olive oil has a magic that defies definition – for me, wonderful, shining mayonnaise is the epitome of good French cooking. The ingredients could not be simpler but they must be the best of their kind: fresh golden-yellow egg yolks from hens that roam the farmyard and sumptuously lipid olive oil from this year's pressing, fat and fruity and a joy to feel, smell and taste. Then these two ingredients are brought together with the skill that all French cooking depends on and which, for many of us, makes the study and practice of it a never-ending, pleasurable experience.

In time everyone develops their own personal way of making mayonnaise. I like to warm the container, the oil and the egg yolks in the sun. I never let any metal come into contact with the sauce, and herbs are the only extra ingredients I add.

This tarragon mayonnaise goes beautifully with cold poached salmon or chicken as well as eggs. It is also well worth trying different fresh herbs, such as finely chopped chives or dill, to flavour home-made mayonnaise for serving with other summer foods.

SERVES 4

8 fresh eggs
a sprig of tarragon
MAYONNAISE
2 egg yolks
300 ml ($\frac{1}{2}$ pint) olive oil
1 level tablespoon chopped tarragon
*extra optional ingredients: mustard, lemon juice
or wine vinegar, salt, freshly milled white pepper*

Hard boil the eggs with the sprig of tarragon for 5−7 minutes or according to their size. Plunge the eggs into cold water and crack their shells.

Warm a bowl and add the egg yolks. Beat with a wooden spoon for half a minute or until sticky. Add one drop of olive oil and beat well. Continue to add oil at this rate until the sauce suddenly changes note while you are beating and you'll see that it has started to thicken.

Now you can add the oil in a fine trickle, providing you continue to beat all the time. If you find that the mayonnaise is getting too thick and doesn't seem to be absorbing the oil, add a teaspoon or so of warm water to thin it. You may find that you do not need all the oil, so stop adding it when you feel that the mayonnaise is right for you. Now taste it and decide if you want to add any of the optional ingredients. Many olive oils provide all the flavour that the sauce needs without any additions.

Mix in the chopped tarragon and spoon the mayonnaise into a bowl. Mayonnaise will keep for 1−2 days, covered in the refrigerator.

To serve the eggs, halve them on to a dish with the cut-side downwards, and spoon the tarragon mayonnaise over the top. Serve with French bread.

TAPENADE

The caper is one of the characteristic flavours of Provence and its ancient Provençal name *tapena* gives the title to this dish. Capers are sold loose from small vats of brine in the markets of the Midi – they are usually on the olive stall.

Tapenade makes a good picnic lunch with a bottle of local red wine and ripe fruit. Serve it in a bowl, surrounded with halved hard-boiled eggs, some crusty country bread and a dish of raw vegetable crudités.

SERVES 4−6

115 g (4 oz) black olives
*50 g (1 $\frac{3}{4}$ oz) tin of anchovy fillets, drained and
rinsed*
4 tablespoons capers, drained
55 g (2 oz) drained tuna fish
1 lemon
100 ml (3 $\frac{1}{2}$ fl oz) olive or sunflower oil
a few extra olives for decoration

Stone the olives and crush in a mortar or chop finely in a food processor. Add the anchovy fillets, the capers, tuna fish and the juice of half the lemon. Either pound or process until you have a fairly smooth paste.

Slowly add the oil to the paste a drop at a time, while stirring, as though you were making mayonnaise. Taste and add more lemon juice if the flavour needs to be sharpened slightly.

Spoon the tapenade into a pottery or wooden bowl, decorate with a few black olives and serve.

ASPERGES À LA FLAMANDE
FLEMISH-STYLE ASPARAGUS

For this version of a classic asparagus dish, I make small bundles of asparagus which I bind loosely with strips of cured raw ham, *jambon cru*. There are many varieties to choose from, either smoked or unsmoked, Italian or French; Parma ham and ham from Bayonne are the best known and easiest to find.

SERVES 4

1 kg (2¼ lb) asparagus
4 slices of jambon cru or Parma ham
2 hard-boiled eggs, shelled
55 g (2 oz) butter, melted
salt and freshly milled pepper
leaves of flat-leaf parsley

Trim any dry or tough ends from the asparagus. Tie the asparagus in a bundle and stand upright in a saucepan containing 5 cm (2 in) of salted boiling water. Cover the tips of the asparagus with a hood of foil, tucking the edges down into the pan. Cook until a sharp knife goes easily into the lower part of the asparagus stalk. Freshly cut young asparagus takes 6–10 minutes to cook, depending on its size, but older and fatter spears might take considerably longer. Drain the asparagus well (keep the cooking water for soup) and divide between four hot individual gratin dishes.

Cut the ham into strips and tie each bundle of asparagus loosely with a strip of ham.

Halve the eggs. Chop the whites, mix with the melted butter and season lightly with salt and pepper. Spoon the mixture over the stalks of asparagus. Push the yolks through a fine nylon sieve and sprinkle them over the whites of egg. Garnish each plate with parsley leaves and serve.

CHAMPIGNONS À LA NIÇOISE
NIÇOISE MUSHROOMS

It is still customary in many regions of France to serve a selection of cold hors-d'oeuvre dishes at the start of a meal. None of the dishes is large but they are all interesting and delicious – some black olives perhaps, and a handful of freshly pulled radishes eaten with sweet butter and crusty bread. There might be a dish of tiny sardines in olive oil, or, in Nice and thereabouts, cultivated mushrooms (*champignons de Paris*) prepared this way with white wine, tomatoes and tarragon.

SERVES 3 – 4

450 g (1 lb) button mushrooms
2 tablespoons fruity olive oil
1 large onion, chopped
1 clove garlic, finely chopped
2 large tomatoes, peeled, seeded and chopped
150 ml (¼ pint) dry white wine
150 ml (¼ pint) water
juice of ½ lemon
salt and freshly milled pepper
1 teaspoon finely chopped tarragon

Wipe the mushrooms with a damp cloth to remove any sand and trim the stalks. Heat the oil in a pan and gently cook the onion until soft. Stir in the garlic and mushrooms. Add the tomato and cook over high heat until the liquid from the tomatoes has evaporated.

Pour in the wine, water and lemon juice and season lightly with salt and pepper. Cook over a high heat until the liquid has reduced to leave just enough sauce to coat the mushrooms. Remove from the heat and stir in the tarragon.

Spoon the mushrooms into a dish and allow to cool before serving.

GNOCCHI AUX ÉPINARDS

GNOCCHI WITH SPINACH

Bright green Provençal gnocchi – airy little dumplings flavoured with spinach and sorrel – flecked with fresh coriander and served with sweet butter and freshly grated Parmesan cheese, make an appetizing first course or they can be served as a main dish.

SERVES 5 – 6

450 g (1 lb) fresh spinach or 225 g (8 oz) frozen
leaf spinach
a handful of sorrel leaves
400 g (14 oz) ricotta cheese or curd cheese
2 egg yolks
55 g (2 oz) grated Parmesan cheese
¼ teaspoon grated nutmeg
salt and freshly milled pepper
55 g (2 oz) plain flour
55 g (2 oz) unsalted butter, melted
1 tablespoon coriander leaves, snipped into pieces

Wash the spinach and place in a pan. Cook for 6 – 8 minutes or until tender in the small amount of water clinging to the leaves after washing. If you are using frozen spinach, cook it according to the instructions on the packet.

Purée the spinach then return to the pan, add the sorrel and stir over high heat until the sorrel is cooked and all the liquid from the spinach has evaporated. Remove from the heat and cool.

Mix the ricotta or curd cheese with the egg yolks, half the Parmesan cheese, and the nutmeg. Add the spinach purée and mix well. Season with salt and pepper. Take a teaspoon of the mixture and shape into a ball. Roll it in the flour and place on a floured plate. Repeat the process with the remaining mixture then chill the gnocchi in the refrigerator for several hours or overnight.

Cook the gnocchi, about 10 at a time, in a large saucepan of boiling salted water. They are done when they rise to the surface of the water after about 4 – 5 minutes. Remove from the pan with a slotted spoon and transfer to a hot serving dish. Cook the remaining gnocchi in the same way.

Mix the melted butter with the chopped coriander and pour over the gnocchi. Sprinkle with the rest of the grated Parmesan cheese.

PISSALADIÈRE

PROVENÇAL ONION TART

These days nearly every small baker in the South of France makes pizza. You buy it cut into squares or baked in the familiar circle. In the part of Provence that borders Italy you'll find this version, made without tomatoes but with plenty of sweet-tasting onions, cooked slowly in olive oil, and a few anchovy fillets and black olives. It is very good and makes an excellent first course or can be taken as part of a picnic meal.

SERVES 10 – 12

DOUGH

225 g (8 oz) strong white flour
1 level teaspoon salt
15 g (½ oz) fresh yeast or 1 level teaspoon dried
yeast
150 ml (¼ pint) warm water
1 tablespoon olive oil

FILLING

680 g (1$\frac{1}{2}$ lb) onions, sliced
2 cloves garlic, finely chopped
3 tablespoons olive oil
50 g (1$\frac{3}{4}$ oz) tin anchovy fillets
12–14 black olives
salt and freshly milled pepper
herbes de Provence

Sieve the flour and salt into a warm bowl. Cream the fresh yeast with half the water, or sprinkle the dried yeast on to the water. Leave in a warm place for about 10 minutes until frothy. Add the yeast mixture to the flour with the remaining water and the oil. Mix well then knead for 5 minutes until the dough feels elastic. Place the dough back in the bowl, cover with a roomy plastic bag and leave in a warm place for about 1 hour or until the dough has doubled in size.

Meanwhile, heat the oil in a pan and add the onions and the garlic. Cover and cook over low heat for about 30 minutes until the onions are soft and mushy but still golden. Remove from the heat and leave to cool.

Turn the dough out on to a floured board and knead gently for 1 minute. Roll out to make a 30 cm (12 in) circle and place on a greased baking sheet. Alternatively, line a greased swiss-roll tin with the dough. Spread the onion mixture over the dough and decorate with the anchovy fillets and the olives. Season lightly with salt and pepper and sprinkle *herbes de Provence* on top.

Leave the baking sheet in a warm place for about 30 minutes until the dough has risen and is slightly puffy. Bake in a very hot oven (220°C, 425°F, gas mark 7) for 25–30 minutes. Serve hot or cold.

HERBES DE PROVENCE *Every market stall in Provence selling herbs and spices will display the mixture of dried herbs – rosemary, sage, thyme, marjoram, basil, fennel, oregano, and mint – known as* herbes de Provence, *in little cloth sacks (often brilliantly coloured), plastic bags, or china pots.*

ROULADE
DE POIRES ET DE POIREAUX

LEEK ROULADE WITH PEARS

The pun on *Pierre et Pierrot* makes this unexpectedly good combination of flavours popular in France. If you prefer, the vegetables can be served simply as purées with another dish, but I like them turned into a roulade to serve as a separate course.

SERVES 6 − 8

ROULADE

450 g (1 lb) leeks, trimmed and washed
115 g (4 oz) butter
1 teaspoon finely chopped mint
salt and freshly milled pepper
a knob of butter
2 tablespoons freshly grated Parmesan cheese
4 eggs, separated

FILLING

680 g (1½ lb) ripe dessert pears, peeled and diced
¼ teaspoon ground cinnamon
115 g (4 oz) curd cheese

Slice the leeks and cook over moderate heat with half the butter until soft and mushy. Purée the mixture in a food processor or liquidizer. Stir in the mint and season with salt and pepper.

Line a swiss-roll tin, 33 × 23 cm (13 × 9 in), with buttered non-stick paper and sprinkle with half the Parmesan cheese.

Mix the egg yolks into the leek purée. Whisk the egg whites until stiff and fold into the purée. Turn the soufflé mixture into the tin and smooth level. Sprinkle the remaining cheese over the top. Bake in a moderately hot oven (190°C, 375°F, gas mark 5) for 10 − 15 minutes until golden and springy.

Meanwhile, melt the remaining butter in a wide pan and cook the pears over moderate heat until tender. Remove from the heat and mash lightly. Season and stir in the cinnamon and curd cheese.

When the soufflé roulade is cooked, carefully turn it out on to a sheet of greaseproof paper and peel off the lining paper. Spoon the pear filling over the roulade and gently roll up from the narrow end. Slide on to a hot serving dish and serve straight away or place in a hot oven for no more than 5 minutes. Serve in slices.

PAUPIETTES
DE FEUILLES DE CAPUCINE

STUFFED NASTURTIUM LEAVES

Nasturtium leaves have an intriguing peppery flavour which makes them an excellent ingredient in a mixed green salad. In this recipe from the great French cookery writer Prosper Montagné, the leaves are stuffed with a mixture of anchovies and herbs and poached in wine. Montagné also includes in his writings a recipe for stuffed nasturtium flowers, once used widely in the cooking of south-west France.

SERVES 4 − 6

24 − 30 nasturtium leaves
1 teaspoon capers, rinsed and chopped
1 small pickled gherkin, finely chopped
1 teaspoon finely chopped parsley
1 teaspoon finely chopped chervil
50 g (1¾ oz) tin anchovy fillets
150 ml (¼ pint) dry white wine
1 tablespoon herb vinegar
a sprig of thyme
1 bay leaf
2 tablespoons olive oil

Cut the stems from the nasturtium leaves.

Mix the capers, gherkin, parsley and chervil together. Cut the anchovy fillets into narrow strips, allowing one strip for each leaf.

Place a little of the herb mixture in the centre of each leaf and cover with a strip of anchovy. Fold in

the sides of the leaf and then roll up like a cigar with the seam underneath. Arrange the stuffed leaves in a shallow pan and pour over the wine and the vinegar. Add the thyme and bay leaf and simmer very gently over low heat or in a slow oven (150°C, 300°F, gas mark 2) for 10–15 minutes.

Transfer the stuffed leaves to a serving dish. Reduce the wine remaining in the pan over high heat until there are about 2 tablespoons left. Discard

MONET'S NASTURTIUMS *The Impressionist painter Claude Monet spent more than forty years at Giverny. He created a haven where his friends could be sure of excellent food, served in matchless surroundings of colour and light.*

the thyme and bay leaf and mix with the olive oil. Pour the dressing over the nasturtium leaves and chill until ready to serve.

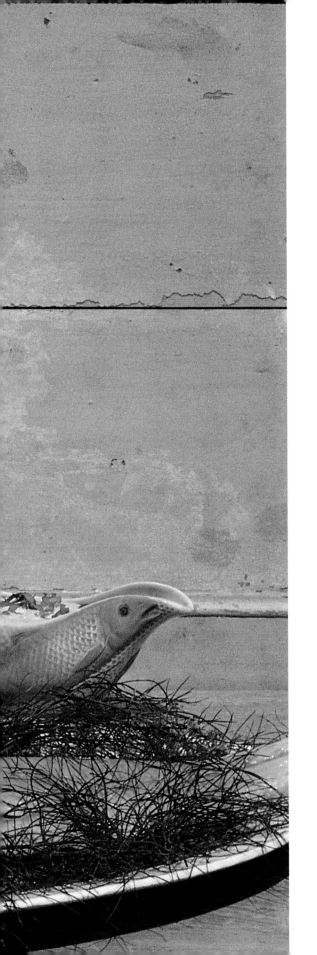

FISH AND SHELLFISH

*It is rare to eat an excellent
dish of fish or shellfish in France
that does not include herbs,
whether the herb is predominant
or a subtle flavour
among many.*

TRUITE DE MER AU FENOUIL ET À LA CRÈME DE
L'OSEILLE *(p. 57).*

Perhaps no other dish illustrates quite so eloquently the skills of fine French cooking as much as fish cooked with herbs. It seems to me that, over the years, I have found remarkably few really delicious fish recipes that call for no herbs at all. Even when a herb is not the predominant flavouring in a dish, I rarely prepare fish without herbs – invariably adding, at the very least, a bay leaf or a little parsley. Not only does the subtle presence of a fresh herb impart a new dimension to the taste of fish, it also, to my mind, appears that we are probably intended to eat the two together. Witness the beneficial effect of sorrel on salmon. The taste of the salmon is given a new depth by the slightly sharp, lemon flavour of the sorrel which, at the same time, makes a rich fish more digestible.

HERB VINEGARS

Most fish cooked in a *bouillon* or a *fumet* benefit from a splash (or what the French call *un filet* – a thread) of an appropriate herb vinegar. These aromatic vinegars also have a role to play in flavouring vinaigrettes, sauces and many other recipes.

Use 3 or 4 sprigs of a fresh herb (see below) to flavour about 500 ml (1 pint) of white wine vinegar. Simply pour the vinegar into a bottle – I like to use one that is attractive enough to be taken to the table for mixing a dressing during the meal. Slide the herbs into the bottle of vinegar, seal the top and leave in a sunny place for 1–3 weeks or until the vinegar has extracted the aromatic oils from the herb. If you wish you can remove the herb although, if it looks pretty, I like to leave it in place.

The principal herbs used for making French herb vinegars are basil, chives, dill, elderflower, fennel, garlic, juniper, lavender, lovage, marjoram, mint, nasturtium flowers, oregano, rocambole, rosemary, sage, savory, tarragon, thyme.

Although it is more usual to make a single herb vinegar, you can produce a more complex aromatic flavour by using two herbs, for example, garlic with oregano. I find the best results are obtained if you add the herbs one at a time. First of all, flavour the vinegar with the garlic, as above. Then strain the vinegar back into the bottle and add the oregano. After 1–3 weeks, either strain off the aromatic vinegar or leave the vinegar in contact with the herb during use.

RASPBERRY VINEGAR

A further refinement is to make a herb-flavoured fruit vinegar. I find raspberry vinegar makes a good background for summer herbs like tarragon, basil and mint. Fill a jar with fresh raspberries and cover with white wine vinegar. Put on a tight-fitting lid and leave in a dark place at room temperature for 3 days. Strain off the vinegar and repeat the process using the strained vinegar but with a fresh batch of raspberries. Strain the vinegar into a bottle. The raspberry vinegar is now ready for use or for flavouring with herbs.

HERB AND WINE INFUSIONS

A final variation on this theme, which need be prepared only a short time ahead, is to make an infusion of wine and herbs for use in a fish *fumet*, *bouillon* or stock, or added in a few judicious spoonfuls to a rich or creamy sauce. Select the wine, preferably a dry white wine, that is to be used in the recipe. Pour the wine into a small bottle with a stopper and add the herbs. Leave in a warm place for 3–4 hours until the wine has absorbed the flavour of the herb.

MERLU À L'ESTRAGON ET À L'ORANGE

HAKE
WITH TARRAGON AND ORANGE

Although I first made this dish using some particularly fine slices of hake, I have since cooked fillets of sole and also whole plaice this way. Simply adjust the cooking time according to the nature and cut of your fish, the method otherwise remains the same.

SERVES 4

4 slices of hake about 2.5 cm (1 in) thick
30 g (1 oz) butter
salt and freshly milled pepper
4 sprigs of tarragon
150 ml (¼ pint) milk
½ teaspoon finely chopped tarragon
½ teaspoon finely grated zest of orange
4 tablespoons double cream

Spread half the butter generously over a shallow ovenproof dish large enough to hold the fish in a single layer. Put in the fish and season lightly with salt and pepper. Place a sprig of tarragon on each slice of fish and pour in the milk. Dot the fish with the remaining butter and cover the dish with a buttered paper.

Cook in a moderate oven (180°C, 350°F, gas mark 4) for 10–15 minutes or until the fish is opaque and is just coming free from the bone. Pour the cooking liquor into a small pan and keep the fish warm, covered by the buttered paper, in the cooking dish or on a hot serving plate.

Add the chopped tarragon and the orange zest to the cooking liquor and simmer for 2 minutes. Stir in the cream and warm through. Taste the sauce and check the seasoning. Spoon the sauce over the fish and serve.

SOLE AU BEURRE DE CITRON VERT

DOVER SOLE
STUFFED WITH LIME BUTTER

The right herb butter can bring out the true flavour of a fish. In this case, zest of lime gives a simple chive butter a hint of piquancy that enhances Dover sole.

SERVES 4

4 Dover or lemon soles
salt
150 g (5 oz) butter, softened
juice and finely grated zest of 1 lime
1 tablespoon chopped chives
2 tablespoons dry breadcrumbs

Remove the heads and dark skin from the fish. Use kitchen scissors to cut off the spiky fins that run along each side. Then use a sharp knife to make a pocket on each side of the backbone by cutting away the flesh from the cross-bones. Lightly salt the fish and place in a buttered ovenproof dish.

Blend 115 g (4 oz) of the butter with the juice and half the zest of the lime. Mix in the chives. Divide the butter between the fish, spreading it into the pockets.

Melt the remaining butter and brush it over the fish. Mix the breadcrumbs with the remaining zest and sprinkle over each fish.

Cook the fish in a moderate oven (180°C, 350°F, gas mark 4) for 25–30 minutes or until just cooked.

BOURRIDE

In nineteenth-century Provence, this glorious garlic-rich fish dish was known as *aïoli-bourride*, its name indicating one of the main ingredients, the wonderful aromatic mayonnaise of the Midi – *aïoli*.

A bourride contains a variety of white sea fish: choose whatever is available from bass, turbot, brill, monkfish, gurnard, sea-bream and conger eel. When I am making this dish for a large family party I sometimes include a few crevettes, a langoustine or two and a handful of mussels to add interest and colour.

SERVES 4−6

1−1½ kg (2−3 lb) fish on the bone
1 litre (about 2 pints) water
150 ml (¼ pint) dry white wine
the white part of a leek, sliced
1 bay leaf
1 head or 1 teaspoon of fennel seed
a few sprigs of thyme
a few parsley stalks
a strip of orange peel
4−5 egg yolks
2−3 cloves garlic, crushed
300 ml (½ pint) olive oil
1 stick celery
salt and freshly milled pepper
freshly cooked shellfish such as crevettes,
langoustines, mussels (optional)
finely chopped parsley
8−12 slices of French bread, toasted

Fillet the fish, remove the skin and cut the flesh into chunks and thick slices.

Make a *court-bouillon* by simmering the heads and bones of the fish with the water, wine, leek, herbs and orange peel for 10−15 minutes.

Meanwhile use 2 of the egg yolks, the garlic and the olive oil to prepare the *aïoli* using the same method as for mayonnaise (see page 38).

Strain the *court-bouillon* into a pan, add the celery and season lightly. Poach the fish, putting the thicker, denser pieces in first, but taking care not to overcook them. Transfer the drained, cooked fish to a large, hot serving dish. Reserve the stock to be added to the sauce.

In another pan, whisk half the *aïoli* with the

remaining egg yolks and 300 ml ($\frac{1}{2}$ pint) of the hot fish stock until it just thickens. Pour the yellow sauce over the fish in the serving dish, arrange the shellfish in the dish if you are including it, and sprinkle the parsley over the top.

To serve, place two or three slices of toast in a

BOURRIDE

soup plate and spoon some of the fish and sauce on top. Serve with the remaining *aïoli*, in a separate dish, and plain boiled potatoes.

CALMARS À L'ÉTUVÉE

STEWED SQUID

In Mediterranean France, squid is usually known and sold as *calmar*, but the more descriptive name, *encornet*, referring to the cornet shape of the fish, also appears. I like to cut the fish into rings and either deep-fry the floured rings for serving hot with a dish of *aïoli* or prepare the squid in a long slow-cook style to this recipe from Alan Davidson's masterly *Mediterranean Seafood*.

SERVES 6

900 g (2 lb) of squid, cleaned
150 ml ($\frac{1}{4}$ pint) olive oil
3 medium onions, sliced
2 cloves garlic, chopped
150 ml ($\frac{1}{4}$ pint) red wine
salt and freshly milled pepper
1 bouquet garni, to include a sprig of fennel
6 tomatoes, peeled and chopped

Cut the body of the cleaned squid into rings about 0.5 cm ($\frac{1}{4}$ in) wide and slice the tentacles.

Heat 120 ml (4 fl oz) of the olive oil in a heavy-based saucepan and then add the onions and garlic. Cook these gently until they start to colour, then put in the squid, followed a couple of minutes later by the wine. Once the wine has bubbled for a minute or two reduce the heat and add the seasoning and bouquet garni. Cover the pan and cook slowly for up to $1\frac{1}{2}$ hours until the squid is tender.

Towards the end of the cooking time heat the remaining olive oil in a small pan and add the tomatoes. Cook until reduced to a purée then season and mix with the squid. Serve straight away.

DIGESTIVE FENNEL *Beds of herbs in early monastic vegetable gardens were usually small and narrow, like this bed in a garden in Normandy, so that the herbs could easily be reached from all sides. Tall, feathery fennel was grown extensively by the monks. The seeds help the digestion – very necessary to a diet consisting largely of beans.*

BAR OU LOUP DE MER FLAMBÉ AU FENOUIL

SEA BASS
FLAMED OVER DRIED FENNEL

Down a winding lane just outside Aix-en-Provence lies the house and studio of the Impressionist painter Paul Cézanne. The upstairs studio is maintained in the state in which he worked: easels hold canvases ready to receive the brush, and gathered together on the table on which Cézanne composed the subjects of his paintings are some fruit, a wine bottle, a jug and a handful of onions – a still life in-waiting.

As you climb the stairs to the studio, you pass an enormous bundle of fennel, its long stalks and flat seed heads pale brown and brittle dry. I wonder, as I gaze at it, whether Cézanne was fond of one of the most superb dishes of Provence where a silver, shimmering sea bass is flamed over a fire of dried fennel. In the Midi, sea bass is known colloquially as *Loup de mer* – sea wolf. It is truly the king of Mediterranean fish.

SERVES 4

700 g – 1 kg (about 1½ – 2 lb) sea bass, scaled and cleaned
a handful of fresh fennel
juice and finely grated zest of 1 lemon
salt
about 4 tablespoons olive oil
2 handfuls of dried fennel twigs
3 tablespoons Pernod

Make 3 or 4 diagonal cuts on each side of the fish and tuck a few fronds of fresh fennel into each cut. Tuck the remaining fresh fennel inside the fish and sprinkle in a little of the grated lemon zest, some lemon juice and some salt.

Brush the fish generously with olive oil and sprinkle with salt. Lay it on an oiled grill rack or in a shaped fish rack. Grill over moderate heat for about 8 minutes each side, basting the fish with more oil during the cooking.

Arrange the dried fennel on a long flameproof dish or tray and lay the sea bass on top. Warm the Pernod in a small pan or a metal ladle and set light to it. Immediately pour it over the fish so that the dried fennel catches light and burns to give the fish its distinctive aroma. Serve straight away.

RAIE AU BEURRE NOISETTE ET AUX CÂPRES

SKATE WITH BROWN BUTTER
AND CAPERS

It is traditional in rural France to serve fish on market day, when gleaming fresh fish is available at one of the travelling stalls. This dish from the classic repertoire of *cuisine bourgeoise* is cooked all over France. In the Midi, though, the capers that garnish the fish will be the superb nonpareil variety, fleshy and aromatic.

SERVES 2

2 wings of skate
85 g (3 oz) butter
1 tablespoon capers, rinsed and drained
1 tablespoon lemon juice or white wine vinegar
1 tablespoon chopped parsley

Rinse the fish in cold water and pat dry.

Melt the butter in a small pan and pour about half of the clear liquid butter into a frying pan. Shallow fry the fish for 3 – 4 minutes on each side and then transfer it to a hot serving dish.

Heat the remaining butter in the small pan until it has just turned pale brown and it smells nutty. Immediately remove it from the heat and stir in the capers, lemon juice or vinegar, and parsley. Spoon the mixture over the fish and serve straight away.

SARDINES AUX FEUILLES DE VIGNE AU PERSILLADE

SARDINES BARBECUED IN VINE LEAVES WITH PARSLEY AND GARLIC

One of the best ways to cook sardines is on a barbecue, each fish wrapped in a bright green vine leaf. If you are able to fuel the flames with vine prunings then the cooked fish will have an unforgettable winey-smoky flavour. Simply place the twigs over the burning fuel just before you start to cook the fish. A good alternative to vine twigs is a bundle of rosemary. In Provence, the mixture of chopped parsley and garlic known as a *persillade* is also served with other grilled oily fish.

SERVES 4−6

1 kg (2¼ lb) very fresh sardines
24−30 vine leaves, depending on size
PERSILLADE
2−3 cloves of garlic
a large bunch of parsley
juice and finely grated zest of 1 lemon
1−2 tablespoons olive oil

Rinse the sardines in cold water then drain well on kitchen paper and set aside in a cold place while you prepare the *persillade*.

Chop the garlic very finely with the leaves of the parsley. Add a little finely grated zest of lemon and moisten the mixture with some lemon juice and olive oil. Spoon the *persillade* into a pot or dish.

Wrap each sardine in one or two vine leaves and place straight on the grill of your barbecue. If you prefer, the sardines can be pan-fried in a little oil over the fire. Cook the fish for 4−8 minutes, depending on size, turning them over once.

Remove from the heat and peel off the vine leaves which will remove the skin of the fish at the same time. Spoon over some of the *persillade* and serve with wedges of lemon and French bread.

CEVICHE DE TRUITE AU MARC ET AU ROMARIN

RAINBOW TROUT MARINATED IN MARC WITH ROSEMARY

Ceviche is a cold fish dish in which the fish is marinated for several hours in an aromatic and acid mixture until the flesh looks cooked. The fish tastes unusually delicious and, not surprisingly, unlike any cooked fish dish. For my version of ceviche I prefer to use pink-fleshed rainbow trout rather than the ordinary kind because the pretty colour is part of the appeal of the dish.

SERVES 6

3−4 rainbow trout, filleted
4 teaspoons sea salt
2 teaspoons sugar
½ teaspoon green peppercorns, coarsely crushed
3−4 sprigs fresh rosemary
2 tablespoons marc de Bourgogne or Irish whiskey
GARNISH
a few extra sprigs of rosemary

Pat the fish dry (do not skin it). Mix the salt with the sugar and sprinkle it over the fish. Arrange half the fillets, skin-side down, on a length of plastic film in a dish. Sprinkle the green peppercorns over the top and lay a sprig of rosemary on each fillet. Pour the marc or whiskey over the fish and lay the remaining fillets on top, skin side up. Wrap the plastic film tightly around the fish and cover with a weighted plate. Chill for 1−2 days.

Unwrap the fish, discard the rosemary and cut each trout fillet into 1 cm (½ in) wide diagonal slices. Arrange the fish on six small plates and garnish with fresh sprigs of rosemary. Serve with thin slices of buttered rye bread.

SARDINES AUX FEUILLES DE VIGNE AU PERSILLADE

TRUITES
AUX·HERBES EN CHEMISE

TROUT STUFFED WITH HERBS
COOKED IN LETTUCE LEAVES

The clear, sparkling rivers of France's mountains produce some of the best trout in the world. In the Ardèche region these fast-swimming fish, that dart into the cool shadows of a river as soon as you spot them, are still known as the *perdrix des eaux douces* – the fresh-water partridge – on account of their fine flavour. I created this recipe to give trout the refreshing flavour of mint; the fish is wrapped in lettuce leaves and parcelled in foil. We enjoy cooking it outside over a fire or barbecue but, of course, the fish can as easily be cooked in an oven.

SERVES 4

4 trout, cleaned and boned
salt
juice and finely grated zest of 1 lemon
55 g (2 oz) slightly dry, white breadcrumbs
1 tablespoon finely chopped parsley
1 tablespoon finely chopped chives
2 handfuls of mint leaves, finely chopped
freshly milled pepper
2 – 3 tablespoons milk
a little sunflower or safflower oil
*1 cabbage lettuce, such as butterhead, with soft
pliable leaves*

Sprinkle the fish lightly inside and out with salt and some of the lemon juice. Set the fish aside on a plate in a cold place while you prepare the stuffing.

Mix the breadcrumbs with the parsley, chives and mint. Add ½ teaspoon finely grated lemon zest and season with salt and pepper. Stir together with enough lemon juice and milk to bind the mixture. Divide the stuffing between the fish, tucking it neatly inside the body.

Wrap 3 or 4 lettuce leaves around each fish, then place each fish in the centre of a piece of lightly oiled kitchen foil and gather the edges firmly together. Put the fish parcels in the refrigerator until you are ready to cook them.

Place the fish parcels directly on the barbecue grill and cook, turning now and again, for 15–25 minutes depending on size. Alternatively, bake them in an oven (180°C, 350°F, gas mark 4).

ORNAMENTAL BAY *It can take 15–20 years to train a bay tree into as perfect a shape as this. Such decorative bays were a feature of elaborate French seventeenth and eighteenth-century parterre gardens laid out with clipped box hedges.*

56

TRUITE DE MER AU FENOUIL ET À LA CRÈME DE L'OSEILLE

SALMON TROUT WITH FRESH FENNEL AND SORREL CREAM

Salmon or sea trout is a particularly fine fish which is shown to best advantage when cooked whole and served cold. Its delicate taste and texture is complemented by the pale green sorrel cream. The completed dish with its garnish of feathery fennel makes a beautiful centre-piece for a buffet lunch or supper party.

SERVES 6–8

1.5–2 kg (about 3–4 lb) salmon trout, cleaned
salt
a good-sized bunch of fresh fennel fronds
150 ml ($\frac{1}{4}$ pint) dry white wine
SORREL CREAM
100 g ($3\frac{1}{2}$ oz) sorrel leaves
$\frac{1}{2}$ teaspoon finely grated lemon zest and juice of $\frac{1}{2}$ lemon
a sliver of garlic, crushed
salt and freshly milled black pepper
300 ml ($\frac{1}{2}$ pint) double cream
a dash of balsamic vinegar or white wine vinegar

Cover your longest oven tray or roasting tin with a double thickness of kitchen foil large enough to enclose the salmon trout. Season the inside of the fish with a little salt and tuck in some fronds of fennel. Make a bed of fennel on the foil and place the fish on it. Lay more fennel on top of the fish and pour over the wine. Enclose the fish in the foil.

Bake in a moderate oven (190°C, 375°F, gas mark 5) for 25–30 minutes depending on the size. The rule is usually to allow 10 minutes cooking time for each 2.5 cm (1 in) thickness of fish at its highest point when lying sideways. The fish is cooked as soon as the flesh is opaque, but remember that it continues to cook a little as it cools. Remove from the oven and set aside for 10 minutes.

Unwrap the fish, transfer to a large serving dish and discard the cooked fennel. Make a neat cut through the skin in a curved line behind the head. Gently pull off the skin, in sections if that is easier, removing the gills but leaving the tail intact. Scrape away any of the fatty grey layer to reveal the pink flesh. Decorate the salmon trout and the dish with sprigs of fresh fennel. Leave it in a cold place while you make the sorrel cream.

Wash and drain the sorrel leaves and cook in a pan over moderate heat until the leaves have softened and all surplus water has been driven off. Beat the sorrel to a purée, sieve it so that it is quite smooth, then mix in the lemon zest and garlic. Beat the cream until it is thick but still glossy, and then gradually fold in the sorrel purée. Season with salt and pepper and add lemon juice and vinegar to taste. Spoon the sorrel cream into a bowl and serve with the salmon trout.

HILLSIDE GARDEN *A terraced kitchen garden overlooks one of the lush green valleys that nestle between the barren plateaux of the region of Quercy in south-west France (overleaf). Ancient, overgrown walls shield the rows of vegetables and herbs, and a tank collects soft rainwater.*

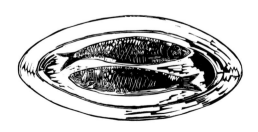

TERRINE DE SAUMON ET DE SOLE AUX HERBES

SALMON AND SOLE TERRINE WITH HERBS

This pretty pink, white and green fish mousse, flavoured with a mixture of herbs, makes a delicious main course for summer lunch in the garden.

The terrine is served with a dressing of oil and vinegar both flavoured with tarragon. This produces a more subtle dressing than the addition of chopped tarragon.

SERVES 4−6

225 g (8 oz) salmon fillet, skinned and cut into long narrow strips

225 g (8 oz) Dover sole fillet, skinned and cut into long narrow strips

225 g (8 oz) fresh spinach

150 ml ($\frac{1}{4}$ pint) fromage frais or small-curd cottage cheese

1 large egg

1 tablespoon finely chopped parsley

2 teaspoons finely chopped chives

1 teaspoon finely chopped tarragon

$\frac{1}{4}$ teaspoon salt

a little freshly grated nutmeg

4−6 tablespoons tarragon-flavoured oil (page 118)

1 tablespoon tarragon vinegar (page 48)

Wash the spinach and cook in boiling salted water for 5−7 minutes until tender but still bright green. Drain well, purée and return to the pan. Stir the purée over moderate heat until all surplus water has been driven off, then cool.

Push the spinach through a sieve then mix the purée thoroughly with the *fromage frais*, egg, herbs, salt and nutmeg.

Line a 450 g (1 lb) loaf tin with lightly oiled vegetable parchment non-stick baking paper. Spoon one-third of the spinach and herb mixture into the tin. Cover with half the strips of fish, add one-third of the herb mixture, then more fish and a final layer of spinach and herb mixture. Cover with a layer of oiled vegetable parchment and cook in a bain-marie in a moderate oven (180°C, 350°F, gas mark 4) for 45−60 minutes until the centre of the terrine is cooked. Cool in the tin overnight.

Turn out and slice. Serve with a dressing made from the tarragon oil and the tarragon vinegar, seasoned lightly with salt.

MOUSSE DE SAUMON À L'ANETH

HOT SALMON AND DILL MOUSSE

A tail-piece of salmon, usually less expensive than a piece cut from the centre of the fish, is fine for making these delicately flavoured little mousses, which are served hot with hollandaise sauce.

SERVES 4

200 g (7 oz) fresh salmon, skinned, boned and chilled

1 egg, chilled

120 ml (4 fl oz) double cream, chilled

salt and freshly milled pepper

$\frac{1}{4}$ teaspoon chopped dill or chervil

a knob of butter

HOLLANDAISE SAUCE

3 tablespoons herb vinegar, flavoured with dill or chervil

6 peppercorns

½ bay leaf

a blade of mace

2 egg yolks

85–115 g (3–4 oz) butter, softened

salt and freshly milled pepper

a few sprigs of dill

Cut the salmon into pieces and place in the bowl of a food processor with the egg and cream. Process for about 3 minutes until the mixture is a thick purée. Season with salt and pepper and stir in the dill or chervil.

Divide the mixture between four well-buttered dariole tins or cocotte dishes and smooth level. Cook in a bain-marie in a moderate oven (180°C, 350°F, gas mark 4) for 15–20 minutes until the mixture has set.

Meanwhile make the hollandaise sauce. Boil the vinegar with the peppercorns, bay leaf and mace until it measures 2 teaspoons. Strain into a bowl and use a wooden spoon to beat in the egg yolks and a small knob of the butter. Set the bowl over hot water over low heat. Gradually beat in the remaining butter, adding a small piece at a time. Do not let the sauce get too hot; plunge the bowl into cold water if it starts to separate. Remove from the heat once all the butter has been incorporated and season lightly. Sometimes I add a very small amount of chopped dill to echo the flavour of the mousse.

To serve, unmould each mousse on to a small hot plate, spoon some hollandaise sauce around it and garnish with a sprig of dill.

FILETS DE SAINT PIERRE AU CERFEUIL

FILLETS OF JOHN DORY WITH CHERVIL

The identifying dark spots on each side of its back give John Dory its alternative name, *Saint Pierre*. According to legend they are the thumb prints of Saint Peter. The fish is particularly prized by French chefs and cooks for its fine texture and flavour.

The fierce appearance of John Dory, with its sharp fins and large head, makes one inclined to cook just the fillets. I either serve this dish just with a few potatoes tossed in chopped mint or I surround the fish with a margin of baby vegetables prepared with green butter as for the Gougère (page 112).

SERVES 4

680 g (1½ lb) fillets of John Dory, skinned

2 tablespoons lemon juice

salt

4 tablespoons hazelnut oil

150 ml (¼ pint) double cream

1 tablespoon finely chopped chervil

½ teaspoon freshly ground coriander seeds

GARNISH

a few chervil leaves

Cut the fillets of John Dory into 3 cm (1¼ in) wide diagonal strips. Sprinkle the fish with the lemon juice and a little salt.

Heat half the oil in a wide pan and gently fry half the fillets for 4–5 minutes or until cooked. Do not overcook or let the fish dry out. Lift out the fish with a slotted spoon and keep hot while you cook the rest of the fish in the remaining oil.

Wipe the pan clean with kitchen paper and pour in the cream with the chopped chervil and the coriander. Bring to the boil and simmer for 2 minutes to extract the flavour from the chervil. Return the fish to the pan and heat through. Spoon on to a hot dish and garnish with the chervil leaves.

ROUGET DE ROCHE PROVENÇALE

RED MULLET
WITH TOMATOES AND OREGANO

In the South of France, red mullet is most commonly known as *rouget de roche*, but the fish also has other names including *apogon*, *barbarin* and *becasse de mer*. The latter translates as sea woodcock because, as with woodcock itself, the liver is left intact for the gamey flavour that it gives to the fish.

SERVES 4 – 6

4 – 6 medium-sized red mullet, scaled and cleaned
3 tablespoons fruity olive oil
1 medium onion, sliced
1 clove garlic, chopped
450 g (1 lb) tomatoes, peeled and chopped
1 green or red pepper, seeded and diced
1 teaspoon sugar
1 teaspoon chopped fresh oregano or $\frac{1}{2}$ teaspoon dried oregano
salt and freshly milled pepper
seasoned flour (optional)
oil for baking or shallow frying

Rinse the fish in cold water and drain on kitchen paper. Heat the olive oil in a pan and cook the onion and garlic until golden. Add the tomatoes, diced pepper, sugar, oregano and a little salt and pepper. Bring to the boil then simmer the mixture for 20 minutes until thickened.

Bake or fry the fish. For baking, brush the fish with oil, place in an oiled ovenproof dish and cook in a moderately hot oven (190°C, 375°F, gas mark 5) for 8 – 12 minutes or until the flesh is opaque. For frying, coat the fish in seasoned flour and shallow fry in oil for 4 minutes on each side.

Arrange the fish in a shallow ovenproof dish and pour over the sauce. Cook in a moderately hot oven (190°C, 375°F, gas mark 5) for 7 – 8 minutes. Serve straight away, or leave to cool and serve cold.

BROCHETTES DE LOTTE AU MENTHE ET AU CITRON

MONKFISH KEBABS
WITH MINT AND LEMON

I created this recipe for cooking on the barbecue in the garden of our French *gîte*. As soon as I get back from the market with the fish I start to prepare the dish, leaving the kebabs to marinate in the refrigerator until we are ready to cook them for mid-day lunch or in the evening, as part of a long leisurely meal spent with local friends and local wine.

SERVES 4

450 g (1 lb) monkfish, haddock or cod, boned
3 tablespoons mild olive or sunflower oil
juice and finely grated zest 1 lemon
2 tablespoons chopped mint
salt and freshly milled pepper
115 g (4 oz) button mushrooms
1 sweet red pepper, seeded and cut into squares

Trim any skin from the fish and cut into 4 cm (1$\frac{1}{2}$ in) chunks. In a shallow dish, mix the oil with the lemon zest and juice, chopped mint, salt and pepper to make a marinade. Turn the fish over in the marinade and chill, covered, for at least an hour.

Thread the fish on to four kebab skewers, alternating the fish with the mushrooms and the squares of red pepper. Brush the vegetables with the remaining marinade.

Grill the kebabs for 10 – 15 minutes, depending on the heat, turning them over now and again. Serve with French bread and a green salad.

HOME PRODUCE *Neat lines of vegetables fill the garden of a cottage nestling against a Normandy hillside.*

SALADE DE CRABE ET DE POULET À MAYONNAISE VERTE

CRAB AND CHICKEN SALAD WITH GREEN MAYONNAISE

Every time I make a green mayonnaise it's different. For me, this is part of its charm. I like my cooking to reflect the seasonality of food, so in the spring the tender new leaves of chives and sorrel go into the sauce. By midsummer the tarragon and chervil plants in my herb garden are at their best and I cannot resist their tantalizing flavour. And then, in the autumn, I use the small, delicate new leaves of marjoram and oregano, hyssop and lovage that have sprouted at the base of stalks gathered earlier.

When I make green mayonnaise while staying in France the herbs I use are those gathered from the hillsides around our home in the Ardèche – serpolet, wild mint and wild fennel. Sometimes my neighbour, Madame Marquet, brings me a bouquet of herbs freshly picked from her garden and these go into the mayonnaise to produce yet another variation on this simple but excellent sauce.

64

SERVES 4

300 ml (½ pint) home-made mayonnaise
a squeeze of lemon juice
¼ teaspoon finely grated zest of lemon
a handful of fresh herbs, according to preference
1–2 tablespoons crème fraîche *or whipped double cream (optional)*
225 g (8 oz) poached or roast breast of chicken, cut in slivers
115 g (4 oz) cooked crabmeat

FOR SERVING

large leaves of a herb like angelica, or lettuce leaves
a few leaves of chervil or flat-leaf parsley

Mix the mayonnaise with the lemon juice and zest. Remove the stalks from the herbs and chop the leaves finely. Stir into the mayonnaise and check the taste. Sometimes I add a little thick cream to round out the flavour.

Gently toss the mayonnaise with the chicken and the crabmeat but do not overmix. Lay the herb or lettuce leaves on four small plates and divide the salad between them. Garnish with the chervil or parsley and then serve.

STEMS TO BE CANDIED *Angelica is farmed throughout the Loire valley and the aromatic candied stems are widely exported. Although the plants will grow as tall as a man, stems for crystallizing are harvested while still young.*

PALOURDES FARCIES AUX AMANDES
CLAMS STUFFED WITH ALMONDS

Although this recipe was intended for clams, particularly the variety from the Atlantic coast of France, it would be equally good made with mussels or the smaller clam known as the *clovisse jaune*.

SERVES 4

40 palourdes or clams
2 tablespoons dry white wine
1 bay leaf
1 slim clove garlic, unpeeled and lightly crushed
85 g (3 oz) butter
55 g (2 oz) ground almonds, lightly toasted
1 tablespoon finely chopped chives
1 tablespoon finely chopped parsley
salt and freshly milled pepper

Scrub the clams and put them in a wide pan with the wine, bay leaf and garlic. Bring to the boil, cover with a lid and cook, shaking the pan over high heat for 1 minute. Remove from the heat and leave the pan, still covered, for 3 minutes.

Transfer the opened clams to four individual gratin dishes, discarding the empty upper shells. Strain the cooking liquor through a very fine sieve.

Cream the butter with the almonds, chives and parsley. Season to taste with salt and pepper and add just enough of the cooking liquor to make the herb butter spreadable. Spoon a little into each clam shell covering the clam completely. Place under a very hot grill and cook until the butter is melted and bubbling. Serve straight away with crusty French bread.

MOULES MARINIÈRE À L'ESTRAGON

STEAMED MUSSELS WITH TARRAGON

The slightly aniseed taste of fresh tarragon gives a fine flavour to the white wine sauce of this classic mussel dish from Normandy. In its most basic form, *moules marinière* is simply mussels steamed in cider or white wine served in soup plates with the wine poured over and chopped parsley added. In a more elaborate version, the sauce is thickened with cream. Here a little butter is whisked in at the last minute.

SERVES 4

2 litres (about 4 pints) mussels
150 ml (¼ pint) dry white wine
150 ml (¼ pint) water
the white part of a leek, finely chopped
a few parsley stalks
a sprig of tarragon
6 crushed peppercorns
salt
45 g (1½ oz) butter
1 tablespoon chopped parsley
2 teaspoons chopped tarragon

Clean the mussels by scrubbing them well under cold running water and pull away the 'beard' of threads from each one. Discard any mussels that do not close completely while you clean them, or any closed mussels that are unnaturally heavy – they probably contain sand or mud that will taint all the others. Drain the mussels in a colander.

Measure the wine and water into a wide pan, add the leek, parsley stalks, tarragon, peppercorns and some salt and simmer for 3 minutes. Add the mussels, shake the pan and then cover with a well-fitting lid. Cook over high heat for 1 minute, shaking the pan now and again. Remove from the heat and leave, covered, for 5 minutes, for the mussels to open in the steam.

Strain the cooking liquor through a muslin-lined colander or a fine nylon sieve to remove any grit. Reject any mussels that have not opened. Turn the mussels into a hot tureen and cover with a cloth. Return the liquor to the clean pan and whisk in the butter over low heat. Add the chopped parsley and the tarragon and pour the sauce over the mussels. Serve with plenty of French bread.

FRUITS DE MER SAUCE VINAIGRETTE

A DISH OF SEAFOOD WITH A HERB VINAIGRETTE SAUCE

A vinaigrette is one of the simplest of the classic sauces of France. For it to have any distinction its principal ingredients must be of the highest quality and because it is served cold with salads, fruits, cold meats and fish, its true flavour is evident with the first mouthful.

At its simplest, a vinaigrette is a combination of oil and vinegar seasoned with salt and pepper. But no good cook is going to let a vinaigrette rest there. I use herb-flavoured vinegar or – and sometimes with – a herb-flavoured oil (pages 48 and 118). A vinaigrette for young vegetables made with a basil oil and an elderflower vinegar is something wonderful.

But no matter if you have none of these aromatic ingredients to hand because this vinaigrette is flavoured with fresh herbs as you prepare it. I find this variation goes admirably with a platter of shellfish like those served in restaurants and cafés around the Normandy coast. Although this dish takes no time to prepare, you wouldn't want to eat it fast; I like to go slowly and accompany the meal with French bread, sweet butter and a bottle of cool Muscadet sur Lie from the Loire valley to bring back memories of many meals like this in northern France.

SERVES 4

1 – 1½ kg (2 – 3 lb) shellfish, ready-to-eat, such as mussels, oysters, clams, cockles and winkles
2 tablespoons herb or plain wine vinegar
salt and freshly milled pepper
120 – 150 ml (4 – 5 fl oz) herb or plain olive oil
1 – 2 tablespoons finely chopped herbs

Arrange the shellfish on beds of chipped ice on four large platters.

Measure the vinegar into a bowl, add the salt and pepper and mix until the salt is dissolved. Gradually mix in the oil and the herbs, stirring vigorously. Divide the vinaigrette between four small dishes and place one in the centre of each platter of seafood. Serve straight away with plenty of crusty French bread.

COQUILLES SAINT-JACQUES MARINÉES AU CITRON VERT ET À L'ANETH

MARINATED SCALLOPS WITH LIME AND DILL

As is the case with oysters, fresh scallops are delicious either cooked or eaten raw. Marinating them in a dressing of lime juice, dill and ginger gives them a hint of spice and makes them taste even better.

SERVES 4

8 fresh scallops
2 tablespoons safflower oil
juice and finely grated zest of 1 lime
½ teaspoon finely chopped fresh dill
1 teaspoon ginger syrup from preserved ginger, or honey
salt and freshly milled pepper
FOR SERVING
4 scallop shells (optional)
a few sprigs of fresh dill

Inspect the scallops and detach the black line of the intestines from each. Rinse the scallops in cold water and dry on kitchen paper.

Separate the corals and cut the thick white part of each scallop into three or four slices. Arrange the slices in a single layer on scallop shells or small plates and add the corals.

Whisk together the oil, juice and zest of the lime, dill, ginger syrup and a light seasoning of salt and pepper. Spoon the dressing over the scallops, making sure that all the surfaces are coated. Set aside in a cold place for 1 hour.

Garnish the scallops with sprigs of dill and serve with thinly sliced and buttered rye bread or light pumpernickel.

MEAT, POULTRY AND GAME

Classic French country dishes have their roots in centuries of fine cooking – the basic methods of preparing meat, poultry and game, most involving herbs, have changed little over the years.

SUPRÊMES DE VOLAILLE AU VINAIGRE *(p. 85)*.

HIGH in the Cévennes in central France, there is a small hotel which, at times, has been my home. For days I have sat, reading and writing, in the garden that overlooks the lovely valley of a bubbling river. Across the track that runs down to the river is a fine kitchen garden with rows of well-tended vegetables and herbs. One side is edged with chives that in midsummer are covered with purple spiky flowers, and in the corner there is a large patch of bright green sorrel.

About half an hour before dinner a young man comes out of the kitchen and crosses to the kitchen garden. He picks lettuce, sorrel and chives, and collects a few sprigs of other herbs to make a bouquet garni. Then he returns to the kitchen to finish preparing the meal.

How long, I wonder to myself, have these vegetables and herbs been grown here? I know that the young man, who is the chef of the hotel, was taught to cook by his mother who, in turn, learnt from her mother. Vegetables and herbs have probably grown here for generations, if not for centuries. Here in rural France tradition is valued.

In 1651 *Le Cuisinier François* by La Varenne, the master of cooking and chef to the Marquis d'Uxelles, was published in Lyons and marked an important stage in the development of French cooking. In this book, which appeared in many editions during the seventeenth century, La Varenne recorded the recipes of the courtly food of the time. The style of writing is delightfully fresh and direct and, even three centuries later, the book is still a pleasure to read. Most of the recipes are for simple, good food which we would happily eat today and consequently La Varenne is seen as the founder of modern French cookery. It is interesting to see how many dishes have come down through the centuries remarkably unchanged. There are recipes for Partridge cooked with Cabbage, Quails wrapped in Vine Leaves and Oeufs à la Neige – all classic dishes of French country cooking today. This is cooking in a genuine tradition, which deserves and, in France, receives, the utmost respect.

BOUQUETS GARNIS

I turned to the chapter in La Varenne on meat, which is prefaced with instructions for cooking meat in a liquid. He describes the bouquet garni that should be added to the pan – a small bunch of parsley, a spring onion and thyme, tied together.

Later authorities offer many variations on this version. A bay leaf might be added, the onion is often replaced with a piece of leek. In the regional cooking of Provence, it is customary to add a strip of orange zest to a bouquet garni for beef. In Gascony a sprig of hyssop is added to the bouquet garni for tomatoes. In some areas of the South of France a clove of garlic might also be included.

The classic bouquet garni which is suitable for most meat dishes consists of 2 sprigs of parsley, 1 sprig of thyme and a bay leaf, tied together with thread long enough to be tied to the handle of the pan so that the bouquet garni can be removed from the dish before serving. In the past, it was thought appropriate, when composing a bouquet garni for meat and game, to consider the terrain on which the animal or bird has grazed. For example, when cooking venison it can be a good idea to include a few juniper berries and perhaps a sprig of rosemary. Here are some further suggestions, but do not regard them as sacrosanct. Do follow your own instinct as well, and gather the herbs you think most suitable, or that please you, for a particular dish. Cooking and eating are, above all, personal pleasures.

CHICKEN AND TURKEY Parsley, chives or leek, thyme and a little celery.
BEEF Parsley, thyme, bay, 2 cloves and, if the dish is from Provence, a strip of orange zest, all wrapped in a curved layer of leek.
LAMB Parsley, lemon thyme or lemon balm, bay and celery.
PORK Parsley, bay, thyme and a small piece of orange zest.
VEAL Parsley, bay, marjoram, a small piece of lemon zest and sometimes a leaf of sage.
GAME Parsley, bay, rosemary and 2 juniper berries, wrapped in a layer of leek.
TOMATOES Parsley, bay and basil, or for Gascon dishes, parsley, bay, chervil and hyssop.
BROAD BEANS Parsley, chives and savory.
PEAS AND MANGE-TOUT Parsley, mint and chives.
ROOT VEGETABLES Parsley, bay, oregano or thyme.
POTATOES Parsley and bay.

DAUBE PROVENÇALE DE BOEUF

BEEF AND WINE STEW FROM PROVENCE

This classic dish of marinated, slowly cooked beef is one of the most delicious ways of serving topside. The flavour of the meat becomes rich and aromatic and, in my view, totally irresistible.

SERVES 5−6

1 kg (2¼ lb) topside of beef
300 ml (½ pint) Côtes du Rhône red wine
3 tablespoons olive oil
1−2 cloves garlic, crushed
1 teaspoon herbes de Provence
salt
6 peppercorns
115 g (4 oz) lard fumé or smoked streaky bacon, diced
1 medium onion, chopped
225 g (8 oz) tomatoes, peeled and chopped
a strip of orange zest
2 anchovy fillets, chopped
2 tablespoons black olives

Trim any fat from the beef. In a bowl large enough to hold the meat, mix the wine with the olive oil, garlic, herbs, some salt and the peppercorns. Add the meat to the marinade and turn it over so that it is well coated. It may be easier to put the meat and the marinade in a plastic bag which can be placed in the bowl when sealed. In this way, the liquid makes better all-over contact with the meat. Leave the meat in a cold place or the refrigerator for 1−2 days, turning it over now and again.

Cook the *lard fumé* or bacon with the onion in a cast-iron casserole until the fat runs. Add the beef and sear lightly all over.

Pour in the marinade with the tomatoes, orange zest and anchovies and bring to the boil.

Cover the casserole with a tight-fitting lid and cook in a warm oven (160°C, 325°F, gas mark 3), for 2−3 hours until the meat is beautifully tender. Add the olives 10 minutes before serving.

Carve the beef into slices and serve with the sauce (reduced over high heat if need be) and a dish of plain boiled noodles.

INGREDIENTS FOR HERBES DE PROVENCE *Bundles of dried herbs − the main constituents of the mixture known as* herbes de Provence *− are laid out for sale in a market.*

MESSICANI D'EDOUARD DE POMIANE

EDOUARD DE POMIANE'S VEAL PAUPIETTES

This recipe for veal seasoned with fresh thyme comes from the inimitable Dr de Pomiane who was a professor at the Institut Pasteur in Paris during the 1930s. His food is always delicious and nearly always quick to prepare. Indeed, one of his cookery books is entitled *Cooking in Ten Minutes*. He prefaces this recipe with the comment, 'These are tiny paupiettes of veal without stuffing. They are cooked in a few minutes and eaten in a few seconds.'

SERVES 6

450 g (1 lb) noix or topside cut of veal
180 g (6 oz) thinly sliced ham
a small bunch of thyme
55 g (2 oz) butter
salt and freshly milled pepper

Slice the veal as thinly as possible, using a very sharp knife. Each slice should be no more than 0.5 cm ($\frac{1}{4}$ in) thick and about the size of the palm of your hand. On each of the slices lay a rather smaller, very thin slice of ham and a few leaves of thyme. Roll them up and secure each of them with a wooden toothpick. You will have about 12 *paupiettes*.

Melt the butter in a cast-iron casserole and arrange the rolls of meat in the bottom. Cook over medium heat for 5 minutes. Turn them over and sprinkle with salt and pepper.

The good doctor ends his recipe: 'Put them on to a hot dish and serve two to each of your guests after they have eaten a generous plate of spaghetti with tomato sauce and cheese. A few leaves of salad and some fresh fruit, and your meal is complete.'

ESCALOPES DE VEAU AUX POIVRONS ROUGE

ESCALOPES OF VEAL WITH SWEET RED PEPPERS

This recipe dates from a wonderful holiday spent in Uzès in Provence. The path that I took to the town made its way across a meadow that was shoulder high with wild fennel. As I returned home with my shopping I would pick a few of the feathery leaves and the lime-yellow flowers to add to a salad or a new dish that I would create for supper, one of which is this combination of veal escalopes with a piquant sauce of wine and red peppers.

As a variation on this dish you can replace the veal with thin escalopes of pork and use fresh dill instead of fennel to give a slightly more subtle flavour.

SERVES 4

4 veal escalopes
salt and freshly milled pepper
30 g (1 oz) butter
1 clove garlic, chopped
1 red pepper, seeded and cut into neat strips
2–3 pickled gherkins, sliced
1 teaspoon chopped fennel fronds
60 ml (2 fl oz) white wine
2–3 tablespoons crème fraîche or soured cream
GARNISH
a little extra fennel, finely chopped

Put the meat on a plate and season lightly with salt and pepper.

Melt half the butter in a pan and sauté the garlic and red pepper for 2–3 minutes. Add the gherkins and fennel and cook for 2 minutes then transfer the contents of the pan to a plate.

Melt the rest of the butter in the pan and sear the escalopes for 3 minutes on each side. Spoon the fennel mixture on top of the meat and add the wine. Cover the pan and cook for 8–10 minutes until the meat is tender. The cooking liquid will have reduced to make the sauce.

Transfer the meat and the sauce to a hot serving dish and spoon the *crème fraîche* over the top. Garnish with the extra chopped fennel and serve with hot buttered noodles.

LA LANGUE DE BOEUF AUX CORNICHONS

TONGUE WITH GHERKINS

In 1929 La Mazille wrote a delightful book, *La Bonne Cuisine du Perigord*, about the good homely food of that lovely region of south-west France. I recommend a lightly cured tongue and a home-made herb vinegar for this recipe adapted from the book. If the tongue is salted, it may need to be soaked overnight in cold water before you cook it – ask the advice of your butcher.

SERVES 6–8

1 cured ox tongue, soaked in cold water as necessary
1 medium onion studded with 6 cloves
6 peppercorns
1 bouquet garni made with 1 bay leaf and a sprig of thyme, tarragon and parsley
1 stick celery, chopped
1 carrot, sliced
SAUCE
3 shallots, finely chopped
1 tablespoon goose fat or butter
1 tablespoon plain flour
300 ml ($\frac{1}{2}$ pint) cooking liquor from the tongue
1$\frac{1}{2}$ tablespoons finely chopped chives
1$\frac{1}{2}$ tablespoons finely chopped parsley
2–3 teaspoons French mustard
1 tablespoon tarragon or chervil vinegar (page 48)
2 small gherkins, finely diced
GARNISH
a few leaves of chervil

Put the tongue in a pan and cover with the cold water. Add the onion, peppercorns, bouquet garni, celery and carrot and slowly bring to the boil. Cover and lower the heat so that the water just shivers – *frémit* – for 3–4 hours until a skewer pierces the meat easily.

About 30 minutes before the tongue is cooked, make the sauce. Cook the shallots in the fat or butter until soft and golden. Stir in the flour for 2 minutes then gradually add the tongue liquor, stirring all the time to ensure that the mixture is smooth. Add the chives and parsley and let the sauce cook gently over low heat for 20 minutes.

Lift out the tongue and skin it, removing any small bones or gristle at the same time. Slice the meat neatly on to a large serving dish and keep hot.

Stir the mustard, vinegar and gherkins into the sauce, spoon over the tongue and garnish.

SAUPIQUET DE JAMBON

HAM IN CREAM AND HERB SAUCE

The *saupiquet*, whose name probably derives from *sauce piquant*, is a classic dish from the Morvan hills in south-west Burgundy. This beautiful area of rolling country-side is famous for its fine cattle, cheese and cream. The piquant sauce in this dish is flavoured with juniper berries and wine vinegar and is finished with cream; it is invariably served with ham.

SERVES 4

4 thick slices cooked ham

4 tablespoons white wine vinegar

3 shallots, very finely chopped

3 juniper berries, crushed

300 ml (½ pint) chicken stock

55 g (2 oz) butter

30 g (1 oz) plain flour

150 ml (¼ pint) dry white wine

150 ml (¼ pint) crème fraîche or double cream

2 teaspoons chopped mixed tarragon and parsley

To make the sauce, measure the vinegar into a small pan, add the shallots and juniper berries and simmer until almost all the vinegar has evaporated. Strain, then mix with the stock and set aside.

In a heavy-based pan, melt half the butter and stir in the flour. Cook, stirring, for 3–4 minutes until foaming and straw coloured. Gradually add the stock and the wine, stirring all the time. Simmer the sauce gently for 30 minutes until the taste is mellow. Strain it into another pan, stir in the cream and heat gently. Remove from the heat and beat in the remaining butter in small pieces.

Place the ham in a buttered ovenproof dish and heat through in a moderate oven (180°C, 350°F, gas mark 4) for 10–15 minutes. Pour over the sauce and replace the dish in the oven until really hot. Sprinkle with the chopped herbs and serve.

JAMBON PERSILLÉ

HAM IN PARSLEY ASPIC

Any Burgundian *charcuterie* has a truly impressive array of ready-to-eat dishes, several of which are different cuts of pork set in jelly. I have a personal fondness for pig's snout, *museau*, served this way. This classic *jambon persillé* of the region is the most esteemed of these jellied dishes, owing to its superb texture and flavour.

Burgundian ham is lightly cured so that the flavour is delicate and the meat is rosy pink. For the best results use an unsmoked (green) ham and a flinty white Burgundy wine like an Aligoté or a Chablis. This attractive dish is excellent for a cold buffet.

SERVES 8–12

3 kg (7 lb) lightly cured and unsmoked ham or gammon

2 calf's or pig's feet, halved

450 g (1 lb) veal bones

1 bottle white Burgundy wine (see above)

2 medium onions, unpeeled

2 sticks celery, chopped

2 carrots, cut into chunks

1 bouquet garni made with 2 bay leaves, thyme, parsley, tarragon and a piece of leek

8 black peppercorns

6 cloves

4 allspice berries

5 tablespoons finely chopped parsley

2 tablespoons finely chopped chives

salt and freshly milled pepper

powdered gelatine (see below)

Soak the ham in cold water, if advised by your butcher or your experience, then drain. Put the ham, calf's or pig's feet and veal bones in a large pan and cover with cold water. Bring to the boil and simmer for 5 minutes. Pour off the water and replace with 570 ml (1 pint) of the wine and cold water to cover. Add the onions, celery, carrots, bouquet garni, peppercorns, cloves and allspice

A LA RENOMMÉE DES HERBES CUITES

BEURRE

ŒUFS

OMAGES

FRUITS
ET
PRIMEURS

ORANGES
ET
CITRONS

VOLAILLES

GIBIER

ROTISSER

95

Au Café St. Honoré

berries and slowly bring to the boil. Cook gently, allowing the water just to shiver – *frémir* – for $2\frac{1}{2}$–3 hours or until the meat is really tender. During the cooking skim off any froth from the liquid using a slotted spoon and top up with cold water.

Remove from the heat and allow the ham to cool in the water for 30 minutes then lift out. Remove the skin and cut all the meat from the bones. Cut the meat into large cubes and mix with the parsley, chives and the remaining white wine. Season with salt and pepper if necessary. Leave in a cold place while you prepare the aspic.

Strain the cooking liquor and reduce it by boiling over high heat until it measures 1.5 litres ($2\frac{1}{2}$ pints). Remove from the heat and check the setting strength by chilling a few tablespoons of the

GILDED SIGN WRITING *Relics of an old provisions shop on the Rue St Honoré in Paris, these signs advertise herbs, fruit and vegetables, meat and game, eggs, butter and cheese.*

liquid until set. If your aspic does not set adequately, add some dissolved gelatine.

Spoon the ham and herb mixture into one large bowl or several small ones, or a rectangular terrine. Pour over enough aspic to cover the meat and chill until set. The dish can be stored in the refrigerator for 2–3 days if necessary.

Turn out the *jambon persillé* and slice, or cut into wedges like a cake, while still chilled. Serve at room temperature for the best flavour. I like to serve it with a small jug of herb vinaigrette as well.

FILET DE PORC FARCI AUX PRUNEAUX D'AGEN

PORK FILLET STUFFED WITH PRUNES

In France, some cuts of meat, principally of pork and rabbit, have been cooked with prunes for generations, particularly in the main prune-producing regions, namely the Touraine and the Perigord. The latter is home to the *pruneau d'Agen*, a large juicy prune produced from plums grown on a *prunier d'ente* – grafted tree – of a variety dating from the time of the Crusades. It has been established in Santa Clara in California, the source of most of the prunes available in Britain.

In France, *pruneaux d'Agen* cost more than other prunes but they are the best for making the lovely confection known as *Pruneaux à l'Armagnac*. My neighbour Madame Marquet prepares prunes this way by first soaking the fruit overnight in lime tea. Then she steeps the drained prunes in armagnac for several months before serving them either with afternoon coffee or at the end of a particularly special dinner.

I created this dish for serving cold. It makes a good buffet dish that can be made 1–2 days ahead.

SERVES 10–12

2 pork fillets (tenderloins)
1 tablespoon lime flowers
300 ml ($\frac{1}{2}$ pint) boiling water
225 g (8 oz) large juicy prunes such as pruneaux d'Agen
salt and freshly milled pepper
450 g (1 lb) best pork sausage-meat
1 slim clove garlic, crushed
4 juniper berries, crushed in a mortar
1 tablespoon chopped chives .
2 tablespoons chopped parsley
2 tablespoons Calvados or dry white wine
1 large dessert apple, cored and diced
55 g (2 oz) walnut halves
1 teaspoon herbes de Provence *(optional)*

Measure the lime flowers into a bowl or jug and pour over the boiling water. Leave to infuse for 10 minutes then strain the lime tea over the prunes and set aside for 3–4 hours until they have absorbed the liquid. Drain the prunes and remove the stones.

Trim any trace of fat from the pork fillets and trim the ends. Make 2 or 3 cuts in the meat to enable you to hammer it out to a thickness of 1 cm ($\frac{1}{2}$ in). Season with salt and pepper.

Make the stuffing by mixing the sausage-meat

with the garlic, juniper berries, chives, parsley, Calvados and apple. Season lightly.

Arrange one-third of the prunes on each pork fillet and place walnuts in the spaces between the prunes. Divide the stuffing between the fillets, spreading it in an even layer. Arrange the remaining prunes on one of the fillets and cover with the other fillet, meat-side uppermost. Tie the layers of meat with string in 5 or 6 places and sprinkle the top of the meat with *herbes de Provence*, if you wish.

FILET DE PORC FARCI AUX PRUNEAUX D'AGEN

Wrap the meat in lightly oiled kitchen foil and chill for up to 24 hours until ready to cook.

Roast the meat in a moderately hot oven (190°C, 375°F, gas mark 5) for 45–55 minutes or until cooked right through. If in doubt use a meat thermometer. Place the meat in a cold place until completely cold, then chill. Serve cut in slices.

CARRÉ DE PORC PROVENÇALE

ROAST LOIN OF PORK WITH WINE AND HERBS

Discovering, as a child, Charles Lamb's essay on roast pork seemed to put the final seal of approval on my favourite meal. When, years later, I first cooked Elizabeth David's recipe for a Provençal version my satisfaction was complete.

GARLIC FAIR *Mountains of garlic are piled on stalls and garlands hang from awnings at the annual Marseilles fair.*

SERVES 4 – 5

1.5 – 2 kg (3 – 4 lb) loin of pork
1 fat clove garlic
salt
150 ml (¼ pint) white or red wine
2 – 3 sprigs of fresh thyme
4 tablespoons chopped parsley
2 tablespoons fine breadcrumbs

Use a sharp knife to cut off the rind from the joint and chine the bones (or ask your butcher to do this for you). Keep the rind. Peel the garlic and cut it into slivers, then slip the pieces between the bones. Rub salt all over the meat and place the joint in a dish. Pour the wine over the meat and add the

thyme to the wine in the dish. Set aside in a cold place to marinate for 2 hours.

Place the rind, fat-side up, in the roasting tin and rest the meat on top. Add the wine marinade and cover the meat with buttered paper or kitchen foil. Roast in a moderate oven (180°C, 350°F, gas mark 4) for about 1¾ hours. If the liquid dries up, add a little water.

Mix the parsley with the breadcrumbs. Remove the paper from the meat, and spread the parsley mixture over the fat side, pressing it down with a knife. Lower the oven to 150°C (300°F, gas mark 2) and cook for a further 35–50 minutes, basting the meat now and again with its own liquid so that the breadcrumbs and parsley form a golden coating over the top of the pork.

BOUDIN BLANC AU PERSIL ET AUX CIBOULETTES

BOUDIN BLANC SEASONED WITH PARSLEY AND CHIVES

French *charcuterie* is justly famed for its high standard and ingenious and appetizing utilization of the pig. Nearly everyone in France serves food from the local *charcutière* at least once a week but, nevertheless, there are still some country people who make their own *saucissons*, terrines and pâtés. Boudin blanc, a light sausage sometimes known as a white pudding, is simple to make. The delicately flavoured filling is a blend of white meats seasoned with green peppercorns, ground mace and fresh parsley and chives. A butcher who makes his own sausages is usually the best source of sausage casing.

MAKES ABOUT 12 SAUSAGES

225 g (8 oz) raw breast of chicken
225 g (8 oz) pork fillet (tenderloin)
225 g (8 oz) belly pork
1 shallot or small onion, finely chopped
150 ml (¼ pint) single cream
55 g (2 oz) white breadcrumbs
2 egg whites
3 tablespoons finely chopped parsley
1 tablespoon finely chopped chives
1–2 teaspoons salt
8 green peppercorns, crushed
¼ teaspoon ground mace
about 4 m (4 yds) sausage skins
strong thread such as button twine
a strip of lemon zest

Use a mincer or food processor to chop the meat finely. Mix in the shallot, cream, breadcrumbs, egg whites, parsley, chives, salt, green peppercorns and mace. Test-fry a teaspoon of the mixture to check the seasoning and adjust if necessary.

Soak the sausage skins in cold water for 2 hours then drain well. Fill the casing either by using a sausage-filling attachment or spoon the filling into a large nylon forcing bag fitted with a 2 cm (¾ in) plain nozzle. Tie one end of the casing with thread. Feed the other end over the nozzle and continue until the tied end of the skin is a few inches from the nozzle. Squeeze about 15 cm (6 in) of filling into the casing leaving a small air space and tie with twine. Tie again, a short length from the first tie, ready for the next sausage. Continue to make all the sausages in this way.

Bring a large panful of water to the boil with the lemon zest. Lower the string of sausages into the pan, and when the water returns to the boil turn down the heat. Poach the sausages for 20 minutes. Prick them as they cook, to release air.

Lift out the sausage string, cool, then snip into separate sausages. Grill or lightly fry in butter until hot all through.

BROCHETTE DE ROGNONS À LA SAUCE PROVENÇALE

BROCHETTE OF KIDNEYS WITH PROVENÇAL SAUCE

In Provence this cold anchovy-flavoured sauce is usually served with grilled meat, fish or cold poultry. But I've found that it also goes well with a platter of crudités as part of an hors-d'oeuvre.

SERVES 4

8 lamb's kidneys
8 slices of smoked streaky bacon
herbes de Provence
olive oil
SAUCE
3 anchovy fillets
2 cloves garlic
2 egg yolks
1 tablespoon cold water
120 ml (4 fl oz) olive oil
juice and finely grated zest of 1 lemon
salt and freshly milled pepper

Halve the kidneys and trim away the cores. Cut each slice of bacon in half, sprinkle with *herbes de Provence* and roll up.

Thread the kidneys and bacon rolls alternately on to flat brochette skewers and brush with olive oil. Sprinkle *herbes de Provence* over the meat. Set aside in a cool place while you prepare the sauce.

Rinse the anchovy fillets in cold water and drain on kitchen paper, then chop roughly. Use a pestle and mortar or a food processor to pound or chop finely the anchovy fillets with the garlic, egg yolks and the cold water, to make a smooth paste.

Now gradually add the olive oil mixing it in well with each addition. Add a little finely grated lemon zest and lemon juice to taste. Season with salt, if necessary, and a little pepper.

Cook the brochettes for 10–15 minutes under a hot grill or over a charcoal barbecue, turning them now and again, until cooked.

Serve with some of the sauce spooned over the meat and hand round the remaining sauce for eating with plenty of crusty bread.

CABRI OU L'AGNEAU AU ROMARIN

KID OR LAMB WITH ROSEMARY

In the regions of France that produce goat's cheese you will usually find kidmeat is prepared according to many of the recipes used for lamb. This dish uses fresh rosemary which has a more delicate, less pungent flavour than the dried herb.

SERVES 4–6

a shoulder of kidmeat or lamb
2 tablespoons olive oil
150 ml (¼ pint) dry white wine
salt and freshly milled pepper
3–4 sprigs of fresh rosemary
2 cloves garlic
150 ml (¼ pint) of white wine vinegar

Bone the meat and then cut into 4 cm (1½ in) pieces. Lightly brown the meat in the oil in a cast-iron casserole. Stir in the wine. Season lightly, cover and cook over low heat for 30 minutes.

Detach the leaves from the stalks of rosemary and chop them finely. Pound in a mortar with the garlic and mix with the vinegar.

Spoon the rosemary mixture over the meat and cook, uncovered, over moderate heat for 10–15 minutes until the vinegar has evaporated. Serve with a *gratin* of potatoes.

GIGOT AU PASTIS

ROAST LEG OF LAMB
WITH ROSEMARY AND PASTIS

This dish is cooked anywhere in Provence where herbs grow wild. I usually collect a small bunch of serpolet (wild thyme) and oregano and add a bouquet of fresh rosemary. Whole heads of garlic roasted alongside the meat make the best accompaniment. The garlic cooks to a soft buttery purée and the flavour is mellow with none of the astringency of the raw herb. Whether cooked outside on a spit or indoors in an oven, the meat is tender and aromatic.

In France the shank bone on a leg of lamb is left in one piece and I find that not only does the roast meat look more attractive this way but it is easier to carve. The ever-practical French even sell a kind of clamp that you can screw on to the end of the shank bone to grip while you carve with the other hand. However, if your oven is not large it may be necessary to have the leg of lamb butchered English-style with the shank bone severed.

SERVES 8 – 10

1 medium-sized leg of lamb
5 cloves garlic, or more according to taste
sprigs of serpolet (wild thyme), oregano or
marjoram, and rosemary
olive oil
salt and freshly milled pepper
150 ml ($\frac{1}{4}$ pint) Pernod or other pastis
GARNISH
sprays of rosemary

Peel the cloves of garlic and cut each one into three or four slivers. Make small slits in the meat and slip the garlic with a leaf or two of the herbs into the slits. Brush the meat with olive oil and season with salt and pepper.

Roast the lamb on a spit or in a roasting tin in a moderate oven (180°C, 350°F, gas mark 4) allowing 20 minutes per 500 g (1 lb) if you like your lamb pink, otherwise cook it until it is done to taste. Allow the meat to rest in a warm place for 20 – 30 minutes, then pour off any surplus fat from the roasting tin.

Warm the pastis in a small pan or a metal ladle, set light to it and pour over the meat. Serve the lamb surrounded by sprays of rosemary, with roast potatoes basted with herb butter (page 26). Serve the juices from the tin separately in a bowl.

A PYRAMID OF HERBS *Wooden boxes, piled one on top of the other, make an impromptu display stand in a Provence market for bunches of herbs and bouquets garnis.*

GIGOT AU PASTIS *overleaf.*

NOISETTES D'AGNEAU AUX OLIVES ET AU FENOUIL

NOISETTES OF LAMB WITH OLIVES AND FENNEL

Several years ago I began marinating lean meat and some fish in oil alone, with no wine. I do this because French oils are so superb that I want the flavour of the oil to remain unchanged in the dish. Moreover, breast of chicken marinated in hazelnut oil, or pork fillet with walnut oil taste delicious.

Recently I have been using herb-flavoured oils in the same way; breast of turkey steeped overnight in tarragon and walnut oil is very good indeed and monkfish marinated in basil and pine kernel oil tastes wonderful. It is well worth experimenting with herb-flavoured oils. They are very simple to make and there is an infinite number of combinations of oil and herb.

SERVES 4

8 noisettes of lamb
4 tablespoons fennel-flavoured olive oil
(see page 118)
8 coarsely crushed green peppercorns
salt
8 fronds fresh fennel
2 tablespoons Pernod or other pastis
20 black olives, preferably from Nyons

Pour the oil into a shallow dish and turn the noisettes over in it to coat them on all sides. Sprinkle with the crushed peppercorns. Cover the dish with plastic film and refrigerate for 6–8 hours or overnight.

Heat a tablespoon of the marinade in a heavy-based frying pan until it is fairly hot. Sear the meat on all sides then season lightly with salt. Remove a small sprig from each frond of fennel and set aside for adding to the dish later. Lay the rest of the fennel on top of the meat. Cover the pan and cook the noisettes, over moderate heat, for 20–25 minutes until tender.

Discard the cooked fennel and transfer the lamb to a hot serving dish. Chop the reserved sprigs of fennel and add them with the Pernod to the cooking juices in the pan. Bubble fast for 2–3 minutes, add the olives and taste to check the seasoning. Spoon the sauce around the noisettes of lamb and serve with boiled new potatoes.

PROVENÇAL OLIVES *Baskets filled with olives of all kinds, black, brown and green, large and small, are sold on a market stall in the town of Uzès in Provence, together with capers, gherkins and peppers. Olives are characteristic of Provençal cooking. Green olives are usually immature – only a few varieties remain green when ripe – the bitterness is soaked out in a solution of potash before they are preserved in brine. Black olives, fully ripe, need no such soaking.*

SUPRÊMES DE VOLAILLE AU VINAIGRE

BREASTS OF CHICKEN WITH VINEGAR

This lovely little dish is adapted from a recipe by the great French chef, Paul Bocuse. Using a herb vinegar develops the flavour even more. I find that a raspberry and tarragon vinegar goes well with red onions, or try a rosemary vinegar with shallots. The important thing is the method – the variations I leave to you.

SERVES 2

2 breasts of chicken, skinned
salt and freshly milled pepper
55 g (2 oz) butter
1 small red onion, finely chopped
2 tablespoons raspberry and tarragon vinegar
GARNISH
2 sprigs of tarragon

Season the chicken lightly with salt and pepper. Melt half the butter in a cast-iron pan, add the chicken and brown lightly on all sides for 3–5 minutes. Cover and cook gently over low heat, or in a hot oven (200°C, 400°F, gas mark 6), for 10–12 minutes until the meat is cooked but is still very tender. Transfer the meat to a serving dish, cover and keep hot while you make the sauce.

Add the onion to the buttery juices in the pan and cook, stirring now and again, for 5–7 minutes or until soft. Pour in the vinegar and cook fast until the liquid is reduced and the sauce is slightly syrupy. Remove from the heat and add the remaining butter.

Slice the chicken elegantly and put on individual plates. Spoon the sauce to one side of the chicken. Garnish with the tarragon and serve.

POUSSIN DU DIABLE À LA SARRIETTE

DEVILLED POUSSIN WITH SAVORY

In Provence, summer savory is regarded as invaluable as rosemary for flavouring barbecue meat. My friends use it generously with poultry and pork that is to be cooked over a wood fire. If there is time, I make an aromatic oil by infusing the herb in the oil a day or so ahead.

SERVES 2

2 poussins
salt and freshly milled pepper
4−6 tablespoons savory-flavoured oil or plain olive oil
2 tablespoons chopped summer savory

Use poultry shears or strong scissors to cut through the backbone of each poussin. Open them out and, if you wish, thread a wooden skewer through the splayed legs to keep each bird flat. Place in a dish or pan and season all over with salt and pepper. Brush the oil over the skin and sprinkle a generous amount of chopped savory on top. Set the poussins aside in a cold place for 2−3 hours for the flavour of the herb to penetrate the flesh.

Cook the poussins over a wood fire or under a hot grill, turning frequently, for 25−30 minutes or until the juices from the leg are clear. Serve with a mesclun salad (page 137).

POULET À L'ESTRAGON

CHICKEN WITH TARRAGON

Chicken cooked with delicately aniseed-flavoured tarragon is a well-established summer dish in every French cook's repertoire. The chicken and cream sauce can be served hot or cold which means that the dish can be made to suit the weather or your inclination.

Be sure to use French tarragon in your cooking. It has a fine, subtle flavour. The variety known as Russian tarragon is coarser, with no scent and a bitter flavour.

SERVES 4−6

1.5−2 kg (3−4 lb) roasting chicken
1 litre (1¾ pints) boiling water
55 g (2 oz) butter, softened
2 tablespoons finely chopped tarragon leaves
salt and freshly milled pepper
60 ml (2 fl oz) dry white wine
1 teaspoon butter blended with 1 teaspoon plain flour to make beurre manié
150 ml (¼ pint) single cream

Remove the giblets from the chicken and make stock with them for another occasion. Place the chicken in a bowl or the sink and pour the boiling water over it. This French trick tightens the skin of the bird which in turn seals in the flavour better. Dry the chicken with kitchen paper.

Blend the butter with half the tarragon and a little salt and pepper. Either place the herb butter in the cavity of the chicken or spread it over the breast meat under the skin. Place the chicken in a cast-iron casserole, pour on the wine, cover and roast in a moderately hot oven (190°C, 375°F, gas mark 5), for 1−1½ hours or until cooked.

Transfer the chicken to a hot serving dish. Stir the beurre manié into the juices in the casserole and cook for 1 minute. Add the cream and the remaining tarragon and cook, stirring, until the sauce has thickened. Pour the sauce over or around the chicken and then serve.

FRENCH TARRAGON *An ancient terracotta pot from Anduze in the Cévennes, surrounded by strawberry plants, is filled almost to overflowing with an abundance of delicately flavoured French tarragon.*

To serve this dish cold, it is best to carve the chicken (I prefer to discard the skin – my cats agree with this policy), and then pour the sauce over the meat and set aside until cool. Serve at room temperature for the best flavour.

SUPRÊMES DE VOLAILLE AU PISTOU

CHICKEN BREASTS STUFFED WITH PISTOU

The rich aromatic mixture of fresh basil, garlic, pine nuts and Parmesan cheese known as pistou is the Provençal version of the famous Genoese pesto sauce. Pistou is not only the natural partner for pasta and summer vegetable soups, it also makes an excellent, unusual stuffing for white meat such as chicken or veal. Breasts of chicken stuffed with pistou are equally good served hot, or cold – sliced to show the bands of colour.

SERVES 4 – 6

4 – 6 (depending on size) chicken breasts, skinned
15 g ($\frac{1}{2}$ oz) basil leaves
3 cloves garlic
2 – 4 tablespoons olive oil
30 g (1 oz) freshly grated Parmesan cheese
2 – 3 slices French bread, crusts removed and turned into breadcrumbs
1 tablespoon pine nuts

Use a wooden mallet to flatten the breasts of chicken slightly. Place each one on a square of lightly oiled kitchen foil.

Chop the basil, garlic and olive oil together in a food processor or pound them together in a pestle and mortar. Add the cheese and breadcrumbs and mix with 2 – 3 tablespoons of hot water to make a spreadable paste. Mix in the pine nuts.

Divide the mixture between the chicken breasts and spread it evenly over the meat. Roll up each breast to enclose the pistou and gather the foil together firmly.

Place the foil parcels in a roasting tin and cook in a moderate oven (180°C, 350°F, gas mark 4) for 30 – 40 minutes. Unwrap and serve each chicken breast with the cooking juices spooned over the meat. Alternatively allow the meat to cool in the foil, then chill and slice when cold.

PÂTÉ DE FOIE DE DINDON AUX FEUILLES DE CUMIN DES PRÉS

TURKEY LIVER PÂTÉ WITH CARAWAY LEAVES

Caraway is an easy herb to grow and its fresh leaves have a more delicate flavour than the dried seeds. However, if necessary, the finely ground seeds can replace the fresh herb in this quick liver pâté.

SERVES 4

225 g (8 oz) turkey livers
100 g (3½ oz) unsalted butter, softened
1 small onion, finely chopped
1 slim clove garlic, finely chopped
2 eggs, hard boiled and shelled
½ dried bay leaf, ground to a powder
2 teaspoons chopped caraway leaves or ¼ teaspoon caraway seeds, finely ground
salt and freshly milled pepper
GARNISH
a few leaves of caraway or flat-leaf parsley

Cut the turkey livers into small pieces. Melt 15 g (½ oz) of the butter in a pan and cook the onion and garlic for 3 minutes. Add the turkey livers and cook over moderate heat, stirring now and again, for 5–7 minutes or until the liver is no longer pink.

Remove from the heat and cool for 5 minutes. Spoon the contents of the pan into a food processor or liquidizer, add the chopped hard-boiled eggs and process the mixture to a smooth paste. Add the powdered bay leaf, caraway leaves or seeds and a little salt and pepper to season. Mix in the remaining softened butter until well combined.

Spoon the mixture into four small cocotte dishes or ramekins and smooth level. Chill the pâté until needed (it can be stored in the refrigerator for 2–3 days), then decorate each pot with a sprig of caraway leaf or parsley. Serve with triangles of hot toast made with wholemeal or rye bread.

OIE RÔTIE SAUCE DE L'OSEILLE ET AUX POMMES

ROAST GOOSE WITH SORREL AND APPLE SAUCE

One Christmas a few years ago, when I found an unseasonably good crop of young leaves on my sorrel plants, I made a sauce for the roast goose and I was really pleased with the combination of a sharp lemony sauce with the rich meat. I had to smile to myself, though, when I recently discovered an old dish from the Perigord for goose with a sorrel sauce. Cooks, it seems, re-invent the wheel – in a culinary sense – all the time.

SERVES 6 – 8

4 kg (9 lb) goose
salt
570 g (1¼ lb) English cooking apples such as Bramleys Seedling
30 g (1 oz) butter
4 tablespoons medium-sweet cider
55–85 g (2–3 oz) sugar
30 g (1 oz) sorrel leaves, shredded

Place the goose on a rack in a roasting tin and sprinkle salt all over the skin. Peel and core the apples and cram the peelings into the body cavity, then truss the bird.

Roast the goose in a hot oven (200°C, 400°F, gas mark 6) for 2 hours or until the juice from the leg runs clear. During the cooking pour off the goose fat once or twice and store in a cold place for use in other dishes. Rest the goose in a warm oven for 30 minutes before serving.

To make the sauce, melt the butter in a pan. Slice the apples and add to the pan with the cider and the sugar. Cook over moderate heat until the apples have collapsed into a soft purée. Add the sorrel leaves to the purée, then remove from the heat.

Carve the goose and serve with the apple sauce and gravy from the juices in the roasting pan.

CANARD AUX PICHOLINES

DUCK WITH PICHOLINE OLIVES

Picholines are a type of olive with a long, oval shape and a distinctive, slightly bitter taste that is most appetizing.

SERVES 6

2 – 2.5 kg (4 – 5 lb) duck
3 tablespoons olive oil
2 medium onions, chopped
1 tablespoon plain flour
3 tomatoes, peeled and seeded
150 ml (1/4 pint) dry white wine
75 ml (2 1/2 fl oz) water
salt and freshly milled pepper
4 bay leaves
3 leaves and stalks of parsley
3 cloves garlic, peeled and bruised
300 g (10 oz) picholine or other green olives

Joint the duck into six pieces. Lightly brown the pieces in half the olive oil in a cast-iron casserole, then drain them on kitchen paper.

Heat the rest of the oil in the casserole and cook the onions for 6–8 minutes until golden and transparent. Stir in the flour, then add the tomatoes, wine and water and stir until well mixed. Season with salt and pepper.

Add the joints of duck to the casserole and tuck the bay leaves, parsley and garlic around them. Cover and cook over low heat for 30 minutes.

Cover the picholine olives with boiling water then drain well. Add the olives to the casserole then cook, covered, for a further 30 minutes or until the duck is done. Serve straight away.

SPRING VINEYARD *Rows of vines (overleaf) – still bare of leaves – surround a church in the Bandol region.*

SENTINEL SHRUBS *Dark juniper bushes stand braced against a Provence hillside. Local cooks use the berries.*

MOUSSE
DE FOIE DE CANARD

DUCK LIVER MOUSSE

If duck livers are difficult to find, this mousse is almost as delicious made with chicken livers. The texture is delightfully light and creamy. I like to serve it with a very smooth, warm herb butter.

SERVES 6

225 g (8 oz) duck livers
4 eggs
4 egg yolks
a sliver of garlic, crushed
¼ teaspoon dried thyme, finely ground
300 ml (½ pint) single cream
150 ml (¼ pint) milk
salt and freshly milled pepper
a knob of butter

HERB BUTTER

15 g (½ oz) parsley leaves
15 g (½ oz) chervil leaves
2 tablespoons chopped chives
30 g (1 oz) watercress or American landcress
100 g (3½ oz) butter, melted
a dash of tarragon vinegar or lemon juice
salt and freshly milled pepper

GARNISH

a few sprigs of chervil

Mince the livers finely in a food processor or mincer. Mix in the eggs, egg yolks, garlic, thyme, cream and milk. Press the mixture through a fine nylon sieve into a jug and season lightly with salt and pepper.

Butter 6 small moulds or ramekin dishes and place a circle of buttered greaseproof paper in the base of each. Pour the mixture into the moulds and stand on a layer of folded newspaper in a bain-marie with warm water deep enough to come halfway up the moulds.

Cook in a warm oven (160°C, 325°F, gas mark 3) for 20–30 minutes until set. Do not overcook or the custard may be spoiled. It is cooked when the blade of a knife comes out clean from the centre.

To make the herb butter, rinse the herbs and watercress in cold water and cook in the water clinging to their leaves for 3–4 minutes until softened but still bright green. Chop them very finely in a processor or liquidizer, with a little water if necessary, to make a smooth purée. Add the melted butter in a trickle and then tarragon vinegar or lemon juice to taste. Season lightly with salt and pepper and spoon into a warm jug or dish.

To serve, run the blade of a knife round each mousse and turn out on to a plate. Spoon a little herb butter over the mousse and decorate with a sprig of chervil.

CANARD SAUVAGE
AU GENIÈVRE

WILD DUCK
WITH JUNIPER BERRIES

When I am in France, I spend much of my time living in a small hamlet in the southern Ardèche. The cottage I use has a vineyard on one side and a rolling field of lavender on the other. Behind the house the hillside is covered with the low-growing *maquis*, or scrub, of Provence. This is where I collect most of the herbs for my cooking – the wild thyme or serpolet, wild mint, rosemary and fennel. The tallest herbs are the grey-green juniper trees and in August I pick handfuls of blue berries from them. Some of these juniper berries go into my French cooking, the rest I bring home to England.

Juniper berries have a unique taste, slightly resinous and reminiscent of gin, of course, because the herb is used in its production. It has an affinity with strongly flavoured meat, especially game.

SERVES 2 – 4

450 – 900 g (1 – 2 lb) wild duck (mallard)
1 carrot, chopped
1 small onion, chopped
1 stick celery, chopped
16 juniper berries
salt
150 ml ($\frac{1}{4}$ pint) chicken stock or water
75 ml ($2\frac{1}{2}$ fl oz) gin
45 g ($1\frac{1}{2}$ oz) butter

GARNISH

watercress

Wipe the duck with a damp cloth. Put the carrot, onion and celery in a roasting tin. If you have the giblets from the duck, add those too. Crush half the juniper berries and place them in the cavity of the duck. Sprinkle salt over the skin.

Rest the duck on the bed of vegetables and roast in hot oven (200°C, 400°F, gas mark 6) for 45 minutes. Pour off the surplus fat and turn the duck over so that it is breast down. Roast for 10 minutes more and then, if it is sufficiently cooked, transfer to a hot serving dish and keep hot.

Pour off all the fat from the roasting tin and add the remaining juniper berries and the stock or water to the pan. Boil fast for 5 minutes, stirring to mix in the pan juices, strain the liquid into a jug and discard the vegetables and giblets.

Pour the gin into the hot pan and set light to it. Pour the strained juices back into the pan and boil fast for 3 minutes until slightly thickened. Remove from the heat and add the butter, in small pieces. Shake until the pieces of butter have all melted and mixed into the sauce.

Carve the duck and garnish with the watercress. Spoon a little sauce over the meat and serve the rest of the sauce separately in a bowl.

PINTADEAU AU VIN ROUGE

GUINEA FOWL COOKED IN RED WINE

The slightly gamey-tasting guinea fowl is deservedly popular in France. In small country towns you can sometimes find a market stall selling a yellow-fleshed breed, each bird cleaned, trussed and ready for the oven. I remember one stall where the farmer's wife also displayed a large, coloured photograph of her black and white speckled flock pecking happily in her farmyard.

SERVES 6

2 kg (4 lb) guinea fowl, jointed
2 tablespoons olive oil
200 g (7 oz) lard fumé or smoked streaky bacon, diced
2 medium onions, finely chopped
2 cloves garlic, finely chopped
1 tablespoon plain flour
1 bottle red wine: Côtes du Rhône or Côtes de Provence
6 fresh bay leaves or 3 dried bay leaves
2 sprigs of thyme
1 sprig of summer savory
salt and freshly milled pepper
570 g ($1\frac{1}{4}$ lb) small cultivated mushrooms

Lightly brown the joints of guinea fowl in the oil in a cast-iron casserole over moderate heat. Transfer the meat to a plate and add the bacon to the oil. Cook until the fat runs, then add the onions and garlic. Stir in the flour for 2 minutes then moisten with some of the wine. Add the herbs and place the meat on top. Season and pour in the rest of the wine. Cover with a tight-fitting lid and cook over a low heat, or in a moderate oven, (180°C, 350°F, gas mark 4) for 30 minutes.

Add the mushrooms to the casserole and spoon the sauce over them. Cover and cook for a further 30 minutes or until the guinea fowl is cooked. If the sauce is too liquid, reduce it in a pan then pour it back into the casserole and serve.

FAISAN À LA VIGNERONNE

PHEASANT IN THE STYLE OF THE VINEYARD OWNER'S WIFE

These days it's good to see that, increasingly, *la vigneronne* might also be the owner of the vineyard. This is an excellent, highly delicious way of cooking what can sometimes be a slightly dry bird. If *Vieux Marc de Bourgogne* is difficult to find, replace it with Scotch whisky – even my French friends would approve.

SERVES 4 – 6

a brace of oven-ready pheasant
salt and freshly milled pepper
4 good-sized sprigs of serpolet or cultivated thyme
55 g (2 oz) butter
4 tablespoons dry white wine
1 small red onion or shallot, chopped
115 g (4 oz) black grapes, halved and seeded
2 tablespoons Vieux Marc de Bourgogne
4 tablespoons crème fraîche *or double cream*

Season the pheasant with salt and pepper and place a sprig of thyme inside each. Melt half the butter in a cast-iron casserole and lightly brown the pheasant all over. Add the wine, cover and cook over low heat or in a moderately hot oven (190°C, 375°F, gas mark 5) for 40 – 50 minutes or until cooked to your preference.

Transfer the pheasant to a hot serving dish. Melt the remaining butter in the pan and cook the onion for 4 – 5 minutes until soft. Add the grapes and cook for 3 minutes. Set light to the marc and pour it into the pan. Simmer the sauce until it is syrupy, then remove from the heat and stir in the cream. Spoon the sauce around or over the pheasant, garnish with the remaining sprigs of thyme and serve.

FAISAN À LA VIGNERONNE

CAILLES CUITES DANS DES POIVRONS

QUAILS COOKED IN SWEET PEPPERS

The idea for this dish came from an old Niçoise recipe for thrushes cooked in green peppers. Quails are much more to my taste and a friend who farms these small delicious birds sells some of them boned. These, naturally, are ideal for this method. Nevertheless, quails still on the bone taste just as good cooked this way. Having bought the quails, I choose sweet peppers – red, yellow, orange or even green – matched for size and just large enough to enclose the little birds.

SERVES 4

4 quails
4 sweet peppers
3 – 4 tablespoons herb-flavoured (page 118) or plain olive oil
4 slim cloves garlic
4 sprigs of the herb that matches the oil
salt
mignonnette pepper (page 96)
4 fresh bay leaves

Use a vegetable knife to cut round the stalk of each pepper and make a hole large enough to remove the seeds and the ribs. Rinse out each pepper with cold water then drain well and trickle a little oil inside the peppers.

Tuck a clove of garlic and a sprig of herb inside each quail. Season the birds with salt and pepper and trickle oil over the skin. Slide each quail inside a sweet pepper and place a bay leaf across the open end tucking the ends in to secure it. Place the peppers in an oiled ovenproof dish and trickle the remaining oil over the top.

Cook in a moderately hot oven (190°C, 375°F, gas mark 5) for 30 – 40 minutes, basting the peppers with the oil now and again, until the meat is cooked. Serve straight away.

PIGEONS AUX TROIS HERBES SUR UN LIT DE RIZ

PIGEON WITH THREE HERBS ON A BED OF RICE

It was on a menu outside a pretty restaurant in Forcal-quier that I first saw a dish called *Pigeons aux Trois Herbes*. I really wanted to go in and try their pigeon but we had already packed a big picnic in the car. So we drove on and lunched at the edge of a meadow in the lovely alpine countryside of Haute Provence. Later that summer I concocted my own *Pigeons aux Trois Herbes* and placed them on a bed of rice. But I still wonder about the taste of that dish in Forcalquier. One day, perhaps, I'll go back and try it.

SERVES 2 – 3

2 plump oven-ready wood-pigeons
3 sprigs each of thyme, rosemary and marjoram
55 g (2 oz) butter
1 thick slice of lard fumé *or smoked streaky bacon*
1 shallot, finely chopped
salt and freshly milled pepper
225 g (8 oz) brown short-grain rice
425 ml ($\frac{3}{4}$ pint) game or chicken stock, or water

Check the pigeons for any errant feathers or down and remove if necessary. Tuck a sprig of each herb into the body cavity of each bird.

Melt the butter in a cast-iron casserole and cook the *lard fumé* or bacon and the shallot for 2 minutes. Add the pigeons and turn them over in the butter until browned all over. Transfer the pigeons to a plate and season with salt and pepper.

Stir the rice into the butter in the casserole, pour in the stock and bring to the boil. Place the pigeons on top of the rice and tuck the remaining herbs around them.

Cover the casserole and cook in a moderate oven (180°C, 375°F, gas mark 4) for 1$\frac{1}{2}$–2 hours until the pigeons are tender and the rice has absorbed all the liquid and is cooked.

FILET DE CHEVREUIL À LA SAUGE

VENISON FILLET WITH SAGE

Sage always seems to me to be the poor relative in the herb garden. We only call on it when really necessary, probably in the deep days of winter when there is little choice of fresh herbs. But in all fairness, the herb has more virtue than solely as a culinary stop-gap.

The ancient Greeks valued sage highly and in Britain the Druids believed that a potion made with the herb could revive the dead. It must be admitted, though, that sage should be used with discretion; just two leaves placed inside a roast duck will perfume the whole carcase during the cooking. I have found that the herb goes well with venison, which can be cooked as quickly as beefs-teak providing you have the right cut.

In the past, mignonnette pepper was a mix of spices – red pepper, nutmeg, coriander, cinnamon, ginger and cloves – used for adding to soups and stews. Now the term usually means coarsely ground white pepper. My version is a mixture of 3 parts black pepper, 1 part white pepper and 2 parts coriander, ground in a mill.

SERVES 3 – 4

300 g (10 oz) fillet of venison
salt
freshly milled mignonnette pepper
55 g (2 oz) butter
1 shallot, finely chopped
4 young leaves of sage, cut in narrow strips
150 ml ($\frac{1}{4}$ pint) soured cream

Cut the venison into strips 0.5 cm ($\frac{1}{4}$ in) wide and season with salt and mignonnette pepper. Melt the butter in a pan and soften the shallot for 2–3 minutes. Stir in the venison and the sage and stir-fry for 5–6 minutes or until the meat is cooked to your preference. Lower the heat and stir in the soured cream. Serve straight away.

LAPIN GRILLÉ
DES HAUTS PLATEAUX

GRILLED RABBIT
IN THE STYLE OF THE HIGH PLATEAUX

The mountainous Auvergne region of central France has many simple and excellent recipes for cooking game. This way of grilling rabbit works particularly well over a wood fire, but the rabbit can be cooked on a barbecue, or even in the oven, instead.

SERVES 4 − 5

1 oven-ready rabbit, cut in two lengthwise
115 g (4 oz) butter, melted
6 short branches of rosemary, the same length as the rabbit
salt and freshly milled pepper

MOUNTAIN HERB *In early summer, the lilac-blue flowers of rosemary bushes colour the mountainous regions of Mediterranean France where the shrub grows wild.*

Brush melted butter over a sheet of double-thickness kitchen foil and lay half the rosemary on it. Brush the rabbit all over with melted butter and season with salt and pepper. Place it on the rosemary and cover with the remaining branches. Gather the foil to enclose the rabbit and rosemary and place the package on a grill or a metal sheet over a wood fire or barbecue. Cook, turning over now and again, for 30−40 minutes until done.

Alternatively the rabbit can be cooked in a moderately hot oven (190°C, 375°F, gas mark 5) for 30−40 minutes. Serve with plenty of hot crusty bread or jacket potatoes.

97

EGGS
AND CHEESE

*The simplest dishes of eggs and
cheese are often the most delicious,
especially when they
have been flavoured with a few
fresh herbs or a pinch of
herbes de Provence.*

FROMAGE DE CHÈVRE À L'HUILE D'OLIVE *left (p. 106)*,
FROMAGE FAISELLE AUX FINES HERBES *right (p. 110)*.

NEARLY every market in the South of France has a stall selling dried herbs and spices. Often the spices are sold from a nest of open-topped wooden boxes, while the herbs are displayed in small fabric sacks, their tops rolled down neatly to display their contents. The colours are subtle and gentle – pale-green dried mint alongside dusty-yellow lime flowers for making tisanes, the grey-mauve flowers and seeds of lavender for scenting sugars, and smoky-grey sage and serpolet for seasoning a daube of beef or for adding to a marinade.

These stalls have a calm, peaceful air about them and I try to make all my other purchases before arriving at this quiet, fragrant oasis in the noisy market. Then, with luck, there's time to linger and chat to the stall-holder while I sniff a herb here or taste a speck of spice here. Jean-Paul runs the herb and spice stall in the busy market at Pierrelatte in the Rhône valley. His father works for the Ducros spice and herb company, so naturally Jean-Paul is highly knowledgeable about the origins and particular qualities of the herbs and spices that he sells. I buy pink peppercorns and galingale, lavender-scented soap and a small sack of *herbes de Provence*.

The mixture of dried herbs known as *herbes de Provence* usually comprises basil, fennel, marjoram, oregano, rosemary and thyme with the occasional addition of mint and sage. It is specially aromatic and I use it generously when cooking outdoors in France and in Britain. Sometimes, in wintry Britain when I have found myself with no herbs at all, I have blessed my sack of *herbes de Provence* for bringing that evocative flavour of the South to a dish. Even if your meal is a simple omelette, or a slice of toasted cheese, in the absence of fresh herbs a few *herbes de Provence*, finely ground and sprinkled over the top, can't fail to raise your spirits.

DRYING HERBS

Although not all the culinary herbs are worth drying – I find parsley disappointing, for instance – those, like bay and rosemary, thyme and marjoram, that do dry well are immensely valuable in the kitchen.

Herbs for drying are best collected just before they come into flower when their aromatic oils are strongest. Make sure that any early morning dew has dried, and pick whole stems, not just the leaves. The herbs can then be tied up in bundles and the leaves have a finer flavour if detached from their stems after drying.

Hang the bundles of herbs in a dry, warm place that is out of direct sunlight, which can fade the colour and flavour. When the leaves are as dry as paper, carefully detach them from the stems, store in screw-top jars and keep in a dark cupboard.

The herbs that dry best include the leaves of bay, catmint, lime flowers, lovage, marjoram, mint, oregano, rosemary, sage, savory, thyme, verbena, serpolet; and the seeds of anise, caraway, coriander, cumin, dill, fennel, juniper and lavender.

HERB GARLANDS

When I want to dry just a few herbs, perhaps as a memento of a particular place or herb garden, I make a herb garland – *couronne d'herbes*. This is a very pretty way of drying and storing herbs. The garland can be hung on the wall in a warm kitchen and sprigs or leaves of the herbs can be detached as needed.

To make a herb garland you will need 60 cm (2 ft) of heavy-gauge florist's wire, about 60 cm (2 ft) of thin florist's wire, 6–8 leafy shoots of bay leaves, 4–6 stems of marjoram, 4 short rosemary stems, 4 heads of fennel or dill flower and some sprigs of other herbs that dry well.

Bend the heavy-gauge wire into a circle about 25 cm (10 in) across and twist the ends together securely. Use the thin wire to bind the stems of herbs to the circle of wire. Arrange the bay leaves as a background and tie the other herbs on top, spacing them attractively.

Make a wire loop on one side for hanging the garland and, if it is to be a present, I add a pretty ribbon bow. Hang the garland in a warm, airy position out of direct sunlight which will cause it to fade.

TARTE AUX HERBES

FRESH HERB TART

Eggs are one of the most perfect partners for fresh herbs. I make this lovely creamy tart in midsummer when I want a light dish that tastes of fresh herbs alone.

SERVES 6

PASTRY

150 g (5 oz) plain flour

a pinch of salt

85 g (3 oz) butter

1 egg yolk mixed with 1 tablespoon milk

FILLING

1 clove garlic

2 eggs and 2 egg yolks

150 ml ($\frac{1}{4}$ pint) single cream

55 g (2 oz) mixed fresh herbs (parsley, chives, chervil, tarragon, sorrel), finely chopped

salt and freshly milled pepper

Sieve the flour and salt into a bowl and rub in the butter. Mix to a dough with the egg yolk and milk. Chill the dough, wrapped, for 30 minutes.

Roll out the pastry to fit a buttered 23 cm (9 in) tart tin. Prick the base lightly and bake in a hot oven (200°C, 400°F, gas mark 6) for 10−15 minutes until the pastry is set but not coloured. Remove the pastry case and lower the oven temperature to 190°C (375°F, gas mark 5).

To make the filling, peel the clove of garlic and spear it on the tines of a fork. Use the fork to beat the eggs with the egg yolks and the cream. (This is Escoffier's trick for giving just a hint of the flavour of garlic to a mixture.) Stir in the herbs and season lightly with salt and pepper. Pour the mixture into the pastry case and bake on a hot baking sheet for 20−25 minutes until the filling is set. Serve the tart hot, warm or cold.

As a variation, I sometimes add a little fried bacon or ham, or some grated Gruyère cheese to the filling before pouring it into the pastry case.

RIGODON

BURGUNDIAN HAM CUSTARD

The name of this baked ham and egg custard seasoned with thyme derives from a dance called rigadoon with light and graceful movements, said to have been created by M. Rigaud, a seventeenth-century dancing master in Marseilles. This dish is a speciality of Burgundy; there is also a sweet version from the region which contains ground spices and chopped hazelnuts.

SERVES 4

200 g (7 oz) jambon cru (such as Parma ham) or smoked bacon, diced

45 g (1$\frac{1}{2}$ oz) butter

5 eggs

45 g (1$\frac{1}{2}$ oz) plain flour

570 ml (1 pint) milk, warmed

salt and freshly milled pepper

grated nutmeg

$\frac{1}{2}$ teaspoon chopped thyme

Gently sauté the ham or bacon until the fat runs. Butter a 1.5 litre (2$\frac{1}{2}$ pint) ovenproof dish and put in the bacon.

Whisk the eggs with the flour until smooth. Gradually whisk in the warmed milk. Season the mixture lightly with salt, pepper and nutmeg and stir in the thyme. Pour into the dish and dot the top with the remaining butter.

Bake in a moderate oven (180°C, 350°F, gas mark 4) for 35−40 minutes or until set in the centre and the crust is golden brown. Allow to cool for a minute or two then serve from the baking dish.

OEUFS EN COCOTTE
À L'OSEILLE

COCOTTE EGGS WITH SORREL

The slightly sharp, lemony flavour of sorrel goes well with eggs, either in an omelette or better still, with eggs baked in cocotte dishes.

SERVES 2 − 4

85 g (3 oz) young sorrel leaves
30 g (1 oz) butter
4 eggs
salt and freshly milled pepper
4 dessertspoons crème fraîche *or single cream*

Remove any stalks from the sorrel and wash the leaves in cold water. Drain well. Melt the butter in a small pan and when foaming add the sorrel. Cook over moderate heat, stirring all the time, for 3 − 5 minutes until you have a thick, smooth purée.

Divide the purée between four buttered cocotte or ramekin dishes. Break an egg into each, season with salt and pepper and spoon the cream on top.

Stand the dishes in a bain-marie and cook in a moderately hot oven (190°C, 375°F, gas mark 5) for 5 − 7 minutes until the white of the egg is set but the yolk is still liquid. Alternatively, the dishes can be cooked on the hob in a covered pan of simmering water. Serve the cocotte eggs straight away with French bread.

RENAISSANCE SORREL *The ornamental kitchen garden, or* potager, *at the château of Villandry in Touraine is composed of nine squares, each laid out in a different geometrical pattern. In one of the squares, flourishing sorrel plants are contained by low, clipped box hedges. The gardens at Villandry, which also include a water garden and an ornamental garden, were first laid out in the sixteenth century. They were uprooted in favour of a romantic English-style garden in the 1880s, but restoration of the original Renaissance design was begun by a new owner at the start of this century.*

OEUFS SUR LE PLAT AU BEURRE DE MONTPELLIER

BAKED EGGS WITH MONTPELLIER BUTTER

As an alternative to an omelette, *oeufs sur le plat* is just about the simplest meal on the menu in many a French café or bar. This dish of baked eggs is particularly good topped with a herb butter. Montpellier butter is an enhanced herb butter named after the fine capital city of the Languedoc region. In Provence, this herb paste is blended solely with olive oil – no butter – and is known as *la pommade verte*. Montpellier butter also goes well with poached eggs – try the French method of poaching the eggs in dry white wine – and many fish dishes. The flavour is improved if it is made a day ahead.

SERVES 3 – 6

6 fresh eggs
a knob of butter
MONTPELLIER BUTTER
*115 g (4 oz) mixed fresh herbs: mainly chervil,
chives and tarragon*
a small handful of young spinach leaves
1 shallot, finely chopped
4 – 5 fillets of anchovy
1 slim clove garlic
1 tablespoon capers
2 small pickled gherkins, finely chopped
salt and freshly milled pepper
grated nutmeg
100 g (3½ oz) butter, softened
60 – 90 ml (2 – 3 fl oz) olive oil
lemon juice

To make the Montpellier butter, blanch the herbs and spinach leaves with the shallot in boiling water for 2 minutes. Drain well and chop finely – ideally in a processor. Add the anchovy fillets, garlic, capers and gherkins and chop well. Season with salt, pepper and nutmeg and blend in the butter. Gradually add the olive oil, mixing well all the time, to make a thick green sauce. Add lemon juice to taste and spoon the butter into a small dish.

Butter a shallow ovenproof dish and break the eggs into it. Season lightly and place in a moderate oven (180°C, 350°F, gas mark 4) for 7 – 10 minutes or until the whites are set but the yolks are still liquid. Serve straight away with some Montpellier butter spooned on top and French bread.

BRIOCHE DE GANNAT AU BEURRE DE CIBOULETTE

CHEESE BRIOCHE WITH CHIVE BUTTER

The remote and beautiful region of the Auvergne in central France has an ancient reputation for fine food and generous hospitality. The region still produces many of the outstanding chefs that work in Paris. Its food is based largely on the magnificent cattle that graze on the endlessly rolling terrain of the Massif Central. The people of the Auvergne claim that the pure, dry air of the region accounts for the quality of their cheeses and *charcuterie* because it encourages a slow maturation which gives them both superb flavour.

This cheese brioche from the Auvergne is usually made with mature Cantal cheese. It is particularly good for a picnic, filled with a salad or served warm with soup.

225 g (8 oz) plain flour
60 ml (2 fl oz) warm water
15 g (½ oz) fresh yeast or 1 teaspoon dried yeast
60 ml (2 fl oz) milk
55 g (2 oz) butter
2 eggs, beaten
115 g (4 oz) grated Cantal or Gruyère cheese
a small knob of butter for the tin
CHIVE BUTTER
115 g (4 oz) butter, softened
2 tablespoons finely chopped chives
a squeeze of lemon juice
salt and freshly milled pepper

Sieve the flour into a bowl and set aside in a warm place. Measure the water into a cup and crumble in the fresh yeast or sprinkle in the dried yeast. Stir and leave in a warm place for about 10 minutes until the mixture is foamy.

Meanwhile warm the milk with the butter until just melted. Make a well in the middle of the flour. Add the yeast and milk mixtures and the eggs, and mix well until a soft dough is formed. Knead on a floured surface for 5 minutes until elastic.

Return the dough to the bowl, cover with a loose plastic bag and leave in a warm place until doubled in bulk.

Turn the dough on to a floured board and knead in the cheese. Roll into a sausage shape to fit a well-buttered 20 cm (8 in) ring cake tin. Set aside in a warm place to prove for 10 – 15 minutes until the dough is level with the rim of the tin.

Bake in the centre of a hot oven (200°C, 400°F, gas mark 6) for 30 – 35 minutes or until the brioche is just shrinking from the tin. Leave in the tin for 5 minutes, then turn out on to a wire rack to cool.

Make the chive butter by blending the butter with the chives and the lemon juice. Season with salt and pepper to taste and spoon into a small pot or dish. Serve with the brioche.

FROMAGE AUX HERBES EN GELÉE

HERB CHEESE IN SHERRY ASPIC JELLY

This is a cool and elegant little cheese dish which is excellent served for lunch or as a first course to a light meal. Use the herbs that you most enjoy. I use a mixture of whatever herbs are in peak condition in my garden at the time I am making the dish.

15 g (½ oz) best quality aspic powder
150 ml (¼ pint) cold water
150 ml (¼ pint) medium dry sherry, preferably Amontillado
a small bunch of leaves of fresh herbs
4 small herb cheeses, such as Boursin
a few leaves of lamb's lettuce or watercress
a little vinaigrette dressing

Sprinkle the aspic powder into the cold water, leave to soften, then heat gently until dissolved. Remove from the heat and stir in the sherry. Cool slightly then pour a thin layer into four small dishes or cups that are just a little larger than the cheeses. Cool until set.

Arrange a few sprigs of the fresh herbs on the aspic layer in each dish and place a cheese on top. Pour over the remaining aspic jelly, dividing it evenly between the dishes, and chill until set.

When you are ready to serve, dip each dish briefly in hot water and turn out the cheese on to small plates. Dress the lamb's lettuce or watercress with the remaining herbs and the vinaigrette and arrange around each cheese. Serve with hot French bread or rolls.

FROMAGE DE CHÈVRE À L'HUILE D'OLIVE

GOAT'S CHEESE PRESERVED IN OLIVE OIL

This is an ancient Provençal way of preserving the summer's goat's cheeses for eating during the winter. Use a fine fruity olive oil and all five herbs for the most richly flavoured result.

If small individual goat's cheeses are unobtainable, use a log-shaped cheese, cut in half, instead.

MAKES 10

10 small goat's cheeses

½ teaspoon black peppercorns

¼ teaspoon white peppercorns

½ teaspoon coriander seed

a sprig of thyme

2 bay leaves

3 fronds of fennel

a sprig of rosemary

2 sprigs of summer savory

1–2 litres (2–3½ pints) olive oil

Select a large glass jar or container attractive enough to serve the cheeses from at the table. Put in the peppercorns and the coriander seed. Arrange the cheeses in the jar, placing the herbs attractively against the glass sides as you go. When the jar is full, pour in olive oil to cover the cheeses. Seal the lid and store the jar in a cold place for at least a month before serving.

You can keep the cheeses longer but their flavour will continue to develop until they taste very strong indeed. Some people prefer them that way but it is an acquired taste.

SALADE D'ENDIVE FRISÉE AU CABRIDOU GRILLÉ

ENDIVE SALAD WITH TOASTED GOAT'S CHEESE

Cabri is the Provençal name for a young goat or kid, and *cabridou* (from *cabri* and *doux*) is the name given to the small pebble-like goat's cheese of Provence. These cheeses are often eaten soft and freshly drained but they are most highly prized after maturing for 3–6 months when they develop a dry, grey crust and a powerful, distinctive flavour.

PARIS HERBS *All along the Quai de la Megisserie in Paris, amid a cacophony of bird calls, shops and stalls sell caged birds, pets and plants including pots of herbs.*

For this recipe the goat's cheese should be about 1 month old, when it is firm enough to melt under the grill and provide a most delicious dressing for the cool, crisp leaves of endive. The cheese is prepared the day before by macerating it in olive oil and fresh savory.

SERVES 4

4 small goat's cheeses or slices of a log-shaped goat's cheese
2 tablespoons olive oil
1 tablespoon chopped summer savory
1 teaspoon black peppercorns, roughly crushed
225 g (8 oz) leaves of endive frisée
a handful of rocket leaves
4 tablespoons walnut or hazelnut oil
a dash of lemon juice or wine vinegar
salt and freshly milled pepper
4 thin rounds of French bread, toasted to make croûtons (optional)
GARNISH
marigold or chrysanthemum petals

Place the cheeses in a shallow dish or in a plastic bag resting on a plate. Add the olive oil, savory and crushed peppercorns and turn over or shake the cheeses so that they are evenly covered with oil. Cover or seal and store in a cool place overnight or for up to 24 hours.

Wash the endive leaves in plenty of cold water and shake dry. Arrange in four salad bowls or plates and distribute the leaves of rocket between the salads. Mix the walnut oil with the lemon juice or wine vinegar and a little salt and pepper and pour over the salad leaves.

Stand the cheeses in a flameproof dish and grill under very high heat for 4–5 minutes until melting, then place a cheese in the centre of each salad and sprinkle the marigold petals on top. Serve immediately.

Because the cheese runs when it is toasted, it is sometimes easier to place the cheese on *croûtons* of French bread before toasting. Then transfer both the cheese and the *croûton* to the salad.

FROMAGE FORT

STRONG CHEESE

Fromage fort is a preserved cheese made by mixing well-seasoned goat cheese with grape spirit. Different regions in the South of France have their own interpretation of this ancient preparation and some families still use recipes handed down for generations. *Fromage fort* is usually made in a special pottery jar and it is traditional to leave a little of the cheese from the previous batch at the bottom of the jar before the newly prepared cheese is spooned on top. According to one French writer on the food of the Ardèche, some families have not seen the base of their *fromage fort* crock for at least fifteen years. As its name implies, *fromage fort* has a pronounced taste.

MAKES ABOUT 225 g (8 oz)

2 matured goat's cheeses
2 fresh goat's cheeses
1 clove garlic, peeled and crushed
a little serpolet (wild thyme) or winter savory, finely chopped
eau-de-vie de marc, or whisky
olive oil
salt and freshly milled pepper

Grate or crumble the matured goat's cheeses into a bowl and blend in the fresh cheeses with a fork. Add the garlic and herbs, then gradually work in marc and olive oil in approximately equal quantities until the mixture has the consistency of thick cream. Check the flavour and season to taste with salt and pepper.

Spoon the cheese into a stoneware pot, preferably one which has a lid, and smooth the top level. Cover with a tight-fitting lid and store in a cold place for at least a month before opening. Serve with hot crusty bread or hot jacket potatoes.

SALADE D'ENDIVE FRISÉE AU CABRIDOU GRILLÉ
(p. 107).

PAIN DE FROMAGE ET AU LIVECHE

CHEESE AND LOVAGE LOAF

A freshly baked savoury loaf, still warm from the oven, makes a good basis for an autumn picnic. Add soft cheese or ham or some thinly sliced pepper salami with a layer of tomato, cucumber or gherkins sprinkled with dill or parsley for a delicious open sandwich. This soda bread is quick to make since it contains no yeast.

MAKES ONE 450 g (1 lb) LOAF

180 g (6 oz) white self-raising flour
½ teaspoon bicarbonate of soda
½ teaspoon salt
115 g (4 oz) wholemeal flour
85 g (3 oz) matured Cheddar or Cantal cheese, grated
2 large leaves lovage, cut in narrow shreds, or ½ teaspoon powdered lovage root
½ teaspoon fresh thyme leaves, finely chopped
1 spring onion, finely chopped
150 ml (¼ pint) buttermilk
2–3 tablespoons warm water
a little extra grated cheese

Sieve the white flour, bicarbonate of soda and salt into a bowl and mix in the wholemeal flour. Stir in the cheese, lovage, thyme and onion and mix to a soft dough with the buttermilk and warm water.

Knead the dough lightly in the bowl and then shape it roughly to fit a well-greased and base-lined 450 g (1 lb) loaf tin. Sprinkle with cheese. Bake in a moderately hot oven (190°C, 375°F, gas mark 5) for 1 hour. Cool in the tin for 5 minutes then turn out.

If you prefer, you can shape the dough into a round, slightly flat loaf and place it on a greased baking sheet. Cover it with an upturned cake tin for the first 30 minutes, then bake for 10–15 minutes further, to make a total of 45 minutes.

For a picnic, wrap the loaf in a cloth while still warm. Otherwise, leave until cold before slicing.

CAMEMBERT FRIT AU PERSIL

DEEP-FRIED CAMEMBERT CHEESE WITH FRIED PARSLEY

I had always thought that this dish of fried Camembert was a relatively recent introduction into French cuisine, until I came upon a reference to it in a nineteenth-century French cookery book. This is one occasion where the milder-flavoured curly-leaved parsley has an advantage over the flat-leaf kind because it is better for deep-frying.

SERVES 2 – 4

1 – 2 firm Camembert cheeses, each weighing
about 225 g (8 oz)
1 tablespoon plain flour
1 egg, beaten
3 – 4 tablespoons fine white breadcrumbs,
slightly dry
sunflower oil for deep-frying
a small bunch of curly-leaved parsley

Cut the cheese into quarters and dust the cut surfaces with flour. Dip each piece of cheese into beaten egg and roll in the breadcrumbs until completely coated. If you wish, the pieces of cheese can now be kept in the refrigerator until you are ready to cook them.

Heat the oil to frying temperature (180°C, 355°F) or until a small cube of bread fries to a golden brown in 1 minute. Fry the cheese in the hot oil until golden brown all over. Drain well on kitchen paper and keep hot.

Make sure the parsley is completely dry. Remove the stalks and add a few leaves at a time to the hot oil. Fry for about 30 seconds until the parsley is crisp but is still bright green. Lift out with a slotted spoon and drain on kitchen paper. Serve as an edible garnish to the fried Camembert cheese.

I like to serve a small pot of sharp fruit jelly such as rowan berry or crab apple with the cheese.

FROMAGE FAISELLE AUX FINES HERBES

FRESHLY DRAINED CHEESE WITH MIXED HERBS

Cheesemaking in France is a strictly regional, often very local affair. Although there are plenty of large-scale commercial creameries producing cheese, the most delicious and individual cheeses come from the small producer or farmer who makes them from the milk of his own cows.

On the whole, the cheeses of the South of France are made from either goat's or ewe's milk. Pierre Androuet, the distinguished French cheese expert, advises one to buy cheese made from the milk of animals that graze in vineyards simply because 'it is the best'.

Elsewhere in France, and particularly in Normandy and the Limousin, the fine dairy herds supply rich, creamy cow's milk for the cheeses of the areas. Some of these are aged in caverns until they develop a powerful and unique flavour. However, all over France freshly drained cheese, *fromage frais*, just a few days – or even hours – old, is valued as a food in itself or as an ingredient in cooking. Given a good supply of milk it is perfectly easy to make this cheese at home. I like to flavour the drained cheese with fresh herbs from the garden and in high summer I decorate the cheese with herb flowers.

UNDER THE SIGN OF THE GOAT *A playing card with the zodiac sign of Capricorn indicates that this Dordogne market stall is selling goat's cheeses: some rolled in herbs or pepper, some wrapped in chestnut leaves, and some dusted with ash.*

MAKES ABOUT 225 g (8 oz)

1 litre (1¾ pints) fresh milk, unpasteurized if
possible, fat content according to preference
1 tablespoon liquid rennet
salt
fresh herbs and herb flowers: thyme, chives,
summer savory, marjoram or lemon balm

Gently warm the milk until it reaches blood heat (37°C, 98°F). Remove the pan from the heat and stir in the rennet. Leave the milk, covered with a cloth, in a warm place until set. How long this takes depends largely on the time of year: in summer the curd forms in about 30 minutes, during cold weather it takes longer.

Line a sieve with a double layer of scalded butter muslin or fine cotton and pour in the curds and whey. Tie the corners of the cloth together and suspend the bundle over a bowl to catch the drips. Leave hanging over the bowl for several hours or overnight until all the whey – *petit lait* – has dripped from the curds – *cailles*.

The soft cheese can be used at this stage, seasoned with salt to taste. When I want a firmer cheese I spoon it into a small basket or a proper French stoneware cheese drainer – *faiselle*. Some of the chopped fresh herbs can be mixed with the cheese before spooning it into the drainer. Leave it overnight in a cold place for a little more whey to drip out.

Turn out the cheese and sprinkle with chopped herbs and decorate with herb flowers.

LA GOUGÈRE AUX PRIMEURS AU BEURRE VERT

CHOUX RING WITH BABY VEGETABLES AND GREEN BUTTER

In Burgundy the traditional accompaniment to a glass of Beaujolais is the cheese choux pastry known as *la Gougère*. Sometimes the pastry is cooked in small heaps that swell up during baking to resemble a cabbage – hence *choux*, or cabbage, pastry – or, as in this dish, the paste is shaped into a ring that puffs up so dramatically in the oven that the inside becomes hollow. Usually this hollow is filled with a savoury sauce containing meat or cheese. But best of all, I think, is a filling of young baby vegetables – *primeurs* – running with a herb butter that is also known as green butter. Choose whichever vegetables are most tender at the time.

SERVES 4 – 6

75 g (2½ oz) plain flour
salt and freshly milled pepper
150 ml (¼ pint) boiling water
55 g (2 oz) butter
2 eggs
55 g (2 oz) Gruyère cheese, finely diced

FILLING

85 g (3 oz) butter
a handful of basil leaves
1 teaspoon finely chopped chives
about 570 g (1¼ lb) mixed baby vegetables such as carrots, mange-tout peas, broad beans, turnips, broccoli florets, spring onions, courgettes, baby sweet corn

GARNISH

a few leaves of basil and flat-leaf parsley

Sieve the flour with a little salt and some pepper on to a sheet of greaseproof paper.

Measure the water into a heavy-based pan and add the butter cut in pieces. When the butter has melted bring the water back to the boil. Remove from the heat and immediately add the sieved flour, then beat, over moderate heat, until the mixture leaves the sides of the pan.

Turn the mixture into a warmed bowl and add the eggs one at a time, beating each in well. Finally stir in all but a teaspoon or so of cheese.

Place spoonfuls of the mixture on a greased baking sheet to form a circle about 25 cm (10 in) across and scatter the remaining cheese over the top. Bake in a hot oven (200°C, 400°F, gas mark 6) for about 35 minutes or until the pastry is well risen and golden brown. It is best not to open the oven door during the first 20 minutes of the cooking time, otherwise the pastry may sink.

When the pastry is cooked, remove from the oven and transfer to a wire tray. Use a long sharp knife to cut the *gougère* into two halves all the way round. Lift off the top to allow the steam to escape. Transfer the pastry to a flat serving dish and keep warm until the filling is ready.

While the pastry bakes, prepare the herb butter. Melt the butter in a small pan, add the roughly chopped basil leaves and the chives and heat gently over low heat for 5 minutes to extract the flavour from the herbs. Tip the mixture into a processor or liquidizer and chop finely. Return to the pan and keep warm until needed.

Trim and prepare all the vegetables separately. Place each kind on a sheet of buttered foil and fold up to make a loose parcel. Arrange the foil parcels in a steamer and cook each vegetable over simmering water until tender.

Turn the vegetables into a warm bowl, pour over the herb butter and toss until coated. Spoon the buttery vegetables into the pastry case, replace the top half and decorate with the leaves of basil and parsley. Serve straight away.

COURONNE DE FROMAGE AUX HERBES

HERB AND SOFT-CHEESE RING

Soft cheese flecked with green is set in a ring mould to make a lovely, light dish for a summer lunch. Use a mixture of herbs for the best flavour.

SERVES 6–8

450 g (1 lb) curd cheese

150 ml (¼ pint) soured cream

225 g (8 oz) cooked spinach, well drained and finely chopped

115 g (4 oz) butter, melted

6–8 tablespoons finely chopped herbs, ideally parsley, chives and tarragon or dill

a sliver of garlic, crushed

55 g (2 oz) slightly dry, white breadcrumbs

2 × 11 g (.4 oz) powdered gelatine

4 tablespoons dry white wine or lemon juice

salt

freshly grated nutmeg

GARNISH (OPTIONAL)

85 g (3 oz) cream cheese

a little creamy milk

sprigs of flat-leaf parsley

Mix the curd cheese with the soured cream, drained and chopped spinach, melted butter, herbs, garlic and breadcrumbs.

Sprinkle the gelatine into the wine or lemon juice, leave to soften, then heat gently until dissolved. Stir into the cheese mixture and season to taste with salt and nutmeg.

Line a 1.5 litre (2½ pint) ring mould with plastic film (don't worry about the wrinkles) and pour in the mixture. Smooth it level and chill until set.

Unmould the cheese ring on to a flat plate. The ring can either be served plain, or decorated with the cream cheese mixed with a little milk until smooth enough to pipe rosettes around the top. Arrange a leaf of parsley between each rosette. Allow the mould to reach room temperature before serving. Cut into 12–16 slices.

Serve with a tomato and basil salad and plenty of crisp French bread.

SOUPE SAVOYARDE

VEGETABLE SOUP WITH MILK AND CHEESE

The Savoie region of France is renowned for its superb cheeses among which are Reblochon, Saint-Marcellin and Gruyère. Not surprisingly the local cheeses are used in the classic dishes of the area including this winter vegetable soup.

SERVES 5−6

55 g (2 oz) green streaky bacon, diced, or 30 g (1 oz) butter
1 medium onion, finely chopped
4 leeks, shredded
1 stick celery, chopped
2 medium potatoes, peeled and sliced
570 ml (1 pint) water
2 sage leaves
salt
570 ml (1 pint) milk
10−12 slices of French bread, toasted or fried in butter to make croûtons
150 g (5 oz) Gruyère, thinly sliced

Sauté the bacon in a saucepan until the fat runs, or melt the butter. Add the onion, leeks and celery, cover and cook gently over a low heat for 15−20 minutes until soft but not browned.

Add the potatoes, water, sage and a little salt and bring to the boil. Cover and simmer for 15 minutes. Bring the milk almost to the boil, in a separate pan and then add to the soup. Check the seasoning and keep the soup hot.

Cover the bread *croûtons* with the cheese and lay two in the bottom of each soup bowl. Pour the soup over them and serve straight away.

COLOURFUL HILLSIDE *Neighbouring fields of sage and lavender create splashes of pink and purple in the Drôme. Sage is grown for medicinal purposes and for making tisanes.*

TARTELETTES AU FROMAGE VERT

GREEN CHEESE TARTLETS

Flavour, texture and temperature are contrasted in this combination of cool herb and cheese filling and warm, sesame-seed pastry. These tartlets make a delightful accompaniment to summer drinks or an alternative to a cheese course in a dinner party.

MAKES 12

PASTRY
55 g (2 oz) wholemeal flour
55 g (2 oz) plain white flour
1 tablespoon toasted sesame seeds
55 g (2 oz) butter
3−4 tablespoons cold water
FILLING
225 g (8 oz) soft curd cheese
1 tablespoon finely chopped parsley
1 teaspoon finely chopped tarragon
1 teaspoon finely chopped chives
2 tablespoons double cream
salt and freshly milled pepper
GARNISH
a few leaves of flat-leaf parsley or chervil

Mix the flours with the sesame seeds and rub in the butter. Stir in the cold water and mix to a soft dough. Chill the pastry for 15 minutes. Roll out on a floured board and then use to line 12 greased patty tins. Prick the bases of the pastry cases and bake in a hot oven (200°C, 400°F, gas mark 6) for 15−18 minutes or until golden and crisp.

Meanwhile, combine the curd cheese with the parsley, tarragon and chives in a food processor or liquidizer until the cheese is well mixed and pale green in colour. Mix in the cream and season.

Spoon the green cheese into the hot pastry cases and decorate with sprigs of parsley or chervil. Serve straight away.

VEGETABLES
AND
SALADS

*Herbs combine more happily with
vegetables than with any
other ingredient – they grow together
successfully in the garden and
then complement each other perfectly
in the kitchen.*

HARICOTS VERTS EN ROBE ÉCARLATE *left (p. 131)*,
SALADE DE POIVRONS AUX PIGNONS ET AU BASILIC
right (p. 136).

Aʟʟ good gardeners are aware of the happy associ-ation of vegetables with herbs. When grown alongside each other, the right herb should help a vegetable to grow better by combatting attacks from harmful insects or disease. Garlic grown between rows of carrots helps to prevent carrot fly, and summer savory planted amongst broad beans stops an invasion of blackfly. As a gardening cook, I find it interesting that companion plants usually combine as well in the kitchen as they do in the garden.

However, I daresay that even non-gardeners associate herbs more readily with vegetables than with any other food. Indeed, at times, the borderline between the two can become quite blurred. When we roast whole heads of garlic around a joint of meat or compose a salad solely from the young sprigs of fresh herbs, then plants that we describe as herbs step into the spotlight as vegetables.

Some vegetable-herb partnerships are well known because they are so successful; the happy marriage of tomatoes with fresh basil, for example, or the combin-ation of summer savory with broad beans. Others are less familiar but equally delicious, such as puréed auber-gines with chopped mint, or courgettes with coriander leaves. These and many others are excellent dishes that depend upon a simple and direct interaction of flavours for their appeal.

HERB OILS

There is, however, another way in which herbs can act beneficially upon vegetables – as a herb-flavoured oil for dressing either cooked, blanched or raw vegetables. In fact, once you've started to make herb-flavoured oils you'll find them so delectable that they will be an in-spiration in your cooking.

Before you start to make these oils it's worth giving some thought to which oils are most harmonious with particular herbs. A delicately flavoured herb such as chervil, say, works best with a mild-tasting oil like safflower or grapeseed. On the other hand, a magnificently well-flavoured herb like basil or tarragon can handle a fruity virgin olive oil admirably.

Further variations of flavour are possible if you add a little zest of lemon, orange or lime to the oil at the same time as the herbs.

The basic method is simple enough. Put 2–3 short stems of your chosen herb into a bottle of vegetable oil. Leave in a warm place for 2–4 days. Strain the oil into a fresh bottle, store the oil in a cool place and use as required. The quantities of herbs given below are for about 500 ml (1 pint) oil.

BASIL Add about 12 leaves of fresh basil to olive oil. This oil goes well with nearly all vegetables and salads, tomatoes, of course, but also sweet peppers and blanched mange-tout peas.

ROSEMARY Add 2 short sprigs of rosemary to sunflower or olive oil. The sprigs of rosemary can be left in the oil if you wish. Use with endive and salads of dried beans.

BAY Add 6 fresh bay leaves or 3 dried bay leaves to safflower oil. Dried bay leaves can be left immersed in the oil, fresh ones should be removed. This oil can be used with all green salads.

DILL Add 4–6 sprigs of fresh dill or 2 heads of dill seed to grapeseed or sunflower oil. This is excellent on green salads and with hot or cold potatoes

GARLIC Add 1–2 cloves of garlic, peeled and bruised, to fruity olive oil. This can be used on all robustly flavoured salads and for dressing many hot vegetables.

'MARJOLAINE' *A coloured engraving of marjoram in flower comes from 'La Flore Medicale' published in Paris in 1814.*

CHOU FARCI

CABBAGE
STUFFED WITH CHESTNUTS

Every French cook has her own version of this homely, comforting dish. A stuffed cabbage is in the French country tradition of cooking with whatever ingredients are to hand. The stuffing could be made from a mixture of ground meat and spices, or it may be simply rice or breadcrumbs combined with fresh herbs, or – if you live in the Ardèche or the Dordogne – whole, peeled chestnuts. Once you have mastered the method it is easy to devise your own delicious fillings.

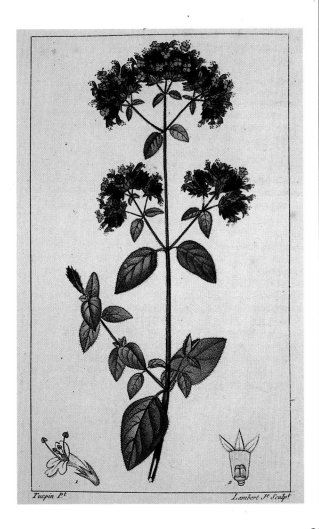

Turpin P.ᵗ   *Lambert Jᵉ Sculpt*

SERVES 4

1 medium to large round, green cabbage
30 g (1 oz) butter
1 small onion, finely chopped
1 clove garlic, chopped
2 dessert apples, peeled and chopped
450 g (1 lb) chestnuts, cooked and peeled
(page 33)
1 teaspoon chopped thyme
½ teaspoon chopped marjoram
salt and freshly milled pepper
a pinch of ground cinnamon
vegetable stock or water
1 bay leaf
a piece of white bread

Discard any damaged outer leaves from the cabbage, cut the stalk level with the leaves and make a cross in it. Wash the cabbage under cold running water, then steam or blanch in boiling salted water for 5–7 minutes or until a knife goes into the centre easily. Lift out the cabbage and leave to cool.

Meanwhile melt the butter and soften the onion, garlic and apple for a few minutes but do not allow to brown. Purée half the chestnuts and halve or chop the rest. Mix all the chestnuts with the onion mixture, the thyme and the marjoram and season with salt, pepper and the cinnamon.

Gently fold back the outer leaves of the cabbage to reveal the centre. Remove some of the centre leaves to make space for the filling. Carefully fold the leaves back over the filling and tie the cabbage together with string.

Place in a casserole and pour in enough stock or water to come half-way up the cabbage. Add the bay leaf and the piece of bread and bring to the boil. Cover the casserole and cook over low heat or in a slow oven (150°C, 300°F, gas mark 2) for 1 hour. Lift out the cabbage, remove the string and cut into wedges for serving. If the cabbage is to be served on its own, it can be accompanied by a herb sauce or herb butter. In France the cooking liquor is served separately, before the *chou farci*, as a soup.

119

COURGETTES AUX FEUILLES DE LA CORIANDRE

COURGETTES WITH FRESH CORIANDER

The influence of the North African countries is still felt in French cooking. A herb much used in Middle Eastern cooking, coriander, is here mixed with ginger and yoghurt to sharpen the slightly bland taste of courgettes.

SERVES 4

450 g (1 lb) courgettes
walnut-sized piece of fresh root ginger, peeled and grated
salt
30 g (1 oz) butter
1 tablespoon roughly chopped fresh coriander leaves
150 ml (¼ pint) Greek sheep's or goat's milk yoghurt

Slice the courgettes thinly and place in a colander or a Chinese steaming basket. Sprinkle the grated ginger on top and steam the courgettes until cooked but not mushy.

Turn the courgettes into a hot serving dish, season with salt and keep warm. Melt the butter in a pan and mix in the coriander leaves and the yoghurt, stirring for 1–2 minutes until hot but not boiling. Pour over the courgettes and serve.

FRUITFUL CENTREPIECE *A standard gooseberry bush and clipped box trees add a formal element to a small herb garden.*

GRATIN DE FENOUIL AU CRABE

BAKED FENNEL WITH CRAB

Florentine fennel is the fat bulbous relative of the herb fennel. I created this recipe one year when it grew specially well in my Devon garden.

SERVES 4

2 large heads Florentine fennel
salt
55 g (2 oz) butter
1 dressed crab
45 g (1½ oz) plain flour
275 ml (9 fl oz) creamy milk
1 bay leaf
55 g (2 oz) Gruyère cheese, grated
1 tablespoon finely chopped oregano
2 teaspoons Pernod or other pastis
grated nutmeg
55 g (2 oz) dryish breadcrumbs
1 tablespoon finely chopped herb fennel

Trim and quarter the heads of fennel. Cook in boiling, salted water for 5–8 minutes or until tender, then drain well. Butter four gratin dishes with 15 g (½ oz) of butter and divide the brown crab meat between them. Arrange the fennel on top and spoon the white crab meat around it.

Melt the remaining butter in a pan and stir in the flour for 1–2 minutes. Then gradually stir in the milk with the bay leaf and cook, stirring, for 5–7 minutes until thickened. Add three-quarters of the cheese with the oregano, Pernod and nutmeg and season with salt. Remove the bay leaf and pour the sauce over the fennel. Mix the remaining cheese with the breadcrumbs and the chopped herb fennel and sprinkle over the top of the dishes.

Bake in a hot oven (200°C, 400°F, gas mark 6) for 10–15 minutes until the breadcrumbs are golden and crisp. Serve with French bread.

TOMATES EN COCOTTE AU BASILIC

CHERRY TOMATOES WITH BASIL CREAM

I created this recipe to make the most of the first cherry tomatoes of the season. If it is possible to make the dish with freshly picked tomatoes and basil from your garden, the flavour is superb.

SERVES 2

10–12 ripe cherry tomatoes
a knob of butter
salt and freshly milled pepper
a few leaves of freshly picked basil
3–4 tablespoons double cream

Cover half the tomatoes with boiling water, prick their skins with a pointed knife then lift out each tomato and peel. Repeat the process with the remaining tomatoes.

Butter two cocotte dishes, ramekins, or very small ovenproof dishes and divide the tomatoes between them, stem-side down. Season with a little salt and pepper and snip the basil leaves into shreds on top. Spoon the cream over the tomatoes.

Stand the dishes on a baking sheet and bake in a hot oven (200°C, 400°F, gas mark 6) for 10–15 minutes until the tomatoes are cooked. Serve straight away with French bread.

TOMATES FARCIES AUX HERBES

TOMATOES STUFFED WITH HERBS

There is a tradition of stuffed vegetables throughout the Mediterranean which Claudia Roden discusses in *Middle Eastern Food*. In Provençal cookery books just about every vegetable has a stuffed version. Sometimes, one vegetable is filled with another, or with herbs or pounded meat or fish. I remember especially one recipe called 'Red Mullet in a Cradle' which involves fitting the fish inside a hollowed-out aubergine.

Firm ripe tomatoes are somewhat easier to stuff. Here they are filled with a mixture of finely chopped herbs blended with creamed Camembert cheese and white wine to make a good picnic dish for serving with cold chicken or ham and a rough country loaf made with rye flour – *pain de seigle*.

SERVES 6

6 medium tomatoes or more if smaller
2 tablespoons olive oil
salt and freshly milled pepper
1 small Camembert cheese, 225–260 g (8–9 oz)
a little dry white wine
3 tablespoons chopped fresh herbs including basil and chervil
½ teaspoon coriander seed, crushed
fine white breadcrumbs (optional)
a few sprigs of parsley or chervil

Cover three of the tomatoes with boiling water, nick the skin with a pointed knife, then lift out and peel. Repeat with the other tomatoes.

Stand the tomatoes on their flatter stalk ends and then cut a lid from the top. Use a teaspoon to remove the insides of the tomatoes: discard the seeds, chop the flesh into a bowl and drink the juice or save it for a soup. Run a little olive oil inside each tomato and season with salt and pepper. Stand upside down on a rack over a plate to catch any surplus oil.

Scrape off the crust of the Camembert cheese and mash the rest into the bowl with the chopped tomato together with a little wine, the herbs and the crushed coriander seed. Mix well, season with salt and pepper and check the flavour. Add more wine or seasoning accordingly. If you think the filling is too moist, mix in some fine white breadcrumbs until it reaches the right consistency.

Spoon the filling into the tomatoes, replace the lids and decorate with a leaf of parsley or chervil. Pour the surplus oil over the tomatoes and serve, or pack into a lidded plastic box for a picnic.

LE POTIRON TOUT ROND À LA MODE DE JULIA CHILD

JULIA CHILD'S STUFFED PUMPKIN

A lovely sight in the Dordogne during autumn is a pile of huge yellow and orange pumpkins sitting at the roadside on their way to the cool cellars in the village. I have found that some winters I can store pumpkins until the spring, but I still think that the best-tasting pumpkins are those that you cook on a misty autumn evening when the leaves are falling and there is a scent of wood smoke in the air.

This recipe is slightly adapted from Julia Child and Simone Beck's delicious baked pumpkin in *Mastering the Art of French Cooking*.

SERVES 6–8

85 g (3 oz) fresh white breadcrumbs
1.8 kg (4 lb) pumpkin measuring about 20 cm (8 in) across
85 g (3 oz) butter
2 medium onions, finely minced or chopped
$\frac{1}{2}$ teaspoon salt
a pinch of freshly milled pepper
a pinch of ground nutmeg
1 teaspoon chopped fresh sage of $\frac{1}{2}$ teaspoon dried sage, powdered
55 g (2 oz) Gruyère cheese, finely diced or coarsely grated
450–600 ml ($\frac{3}{4}$–1 pint) single cream
1 bay leaf

Dry the breadcrumbs on a baking sheet in a slow oven (150°C, 300°F, gas mark 2) for 15 minutes.

Meanwhile, wash and dry the pumpkin. Cut a lid about 10 cm (4 in) across from the top. Scoop out the seeds and stringy flesh and discard. Place in a buttered baking dish or tin.

Melt the butter in a pan and cook the onions over low heat for 8–10 minutes until translucent. Stir in the breadcrumbs for 2 minutes then add the salt, pepper, nutmeg and sage. Remove from the heat and stir in the cheese. Spoon the mixture into the pumpkin and pour in enough cream to come to within 1 cm ($\frac{1}{2}$ in) of the rim. Lay the bay leaf on the top and fit the lid back on the pumpkin.

Bake in a hot oven (200°C, 400°F, gas mark 6) for about 1$\frac{1}{2}$ hours until the outside of the pumpkin is beginning to soften. Lower the oven temperature to 180°C (350°F, gas mark 4) and bake for 30 minutes until the flesh is tender. If the pumpkin is browning, cover it loosely with foil.

To serve, remove the lid and scoop filling and pumpkin into a dish.

WINE AND FRAGRANCE *The brilliant green of rows of vines (overleaf), crossed by the lengthening shadows of a hot Provençal afternoon, contrasts with a vivid field of lavender.*

JALOUSIE D'ÉTÉ

SUMMER VEGETABLE JALOUSIE

Jalousie is the French name for the louvred wooden shutters still to be seen on many houses in the South of France. A sweet pastry with a lid cut into narrow strips has also been given the name because of its shape. I have adapted the idea to make a flat loaf, filled with vegetables and herbs, that is good for taking on a picnic.

SERVES 4−6

FILLING

3 tablespoons olive oil
1 small onion, chopped
1 clove garlic, chopped
1 large tomato, diced
½ red pepper, seeded and diced
½ green pepper, seeded and diced
1 small courgette, sliced
1 baby carrot, sliced and blanched
a few florets of cauliflower, blanched
1 stick celery, diced and blanched
1 tablespoon chopped parsley
a few sprigs of fennel or lovage, chopped
salt and freshly milled pepper

BREAD

340 g (12 oz) 85% wheatmeal flour
55 g (2 oz) buckwheat or rye flour
1½ level teaspoons salt
1 tablespoon olive oil
15 g (½ oz) sachet of easy-blend dried yeast
300 ml (½ pint) warm water
poppy seeds or caraway seeds

To make the filling, heat 2 tablespoons of oil in a pan and cook the onion and garlic until soft and transparent. Add the tomato, peppers and courgette and cook, stirring occasionally, for 5 minutes. Stir in the remaining vegetables and cook for 4 minutes. Remove from the heat, add the herbs and seasoning. Set aside to cool.

Mix the flours with the salt and yeast. Add 1 tablespoon olive oil and mix to a soft dough with the water. Turn the dough on to a floured board and knead for 10 minutes.

Roll out the dough to make a 30 × 23 cm (12 × 9 in) rectangle. Position it so that the short edges are top and bottom. Take the right-hand long edge and fold the dough lengthwise so that the edge now lies down the centre line. Make horizontal cuts just over 2.5 cm (1 in) long across the folded edge of the dough at 2.5 cm (1 in) intervals as though you were cutting a frill. Open out the dough. Spread the filling over the uncut left half. Fold over the slatted right half, pressing the joins together. Brush the top with water and sprinkle with poppy or caraway seeds.

Place the loaf on a large oiled baking sheet and leave to prove in a warm place for 45 minutes. Bake in a very hot oven (220°C, 425°F, gas mark 7) for 20−25 minutes until the top is golden brown and the underside of the loaf sounds hollow when tapped. Transfer to a wire rack and brush the top with the remaining olive oil. Serve warm or cold.

MOUSSE DE PERSIL À LA CRÈME DE CIBOULETTES

HOT PARSLEY MOUSSE WITH CHIVE CREAM

Flat-leaf parsley, which has a finer flavour than the curly variety, is the best kind to use in this delicate mousse served with a hot chive cream sauce.

SERVES 4

a large bunch of fresh flat-leaf parsley
6 tablespoons creamy milk
1 slice of onion
115 g (4 oz) fromage frais
2 large eggs
½ teaspoon finely chopped chives
salt
a small knob of butter
CHIVE CREAM
150 ml (¼ pint) double cream
2 tablespoons finely chopped chives
juice and finely grated zest of ½ lemon
GARNISH
4 leaves flat-leaf parsley

Take 30 g (1 oz) of leaves from the bunch of parsley. Chop finely and set aside. Roughly chop the stalks and any remaining leaves and simmer in the milk with the onion for 3 minutes. Strain the milk on to the finely chopped parsley and cool.

Whisk the *fromage frais* with the eggs, the parsley milk, the chives and add a little salt to season. Pour into four small, buttered, cocotte dishes, ramekins or dariole moulds – the mixture should come about two-thirds of the way up the dish.

Cook the mousses in a bain-marie of hot water in a moderate oven (180°C, 350°F, gas mark 4) for 20–25 minutes until set. Remove from the oven and allow the mousses to cool for 3–4 minutes before turning out.

Meanwhile whisk the cream with the chives until stiff. Fold in the strained lemon juice and ¼ teaspoon of finely grated zest. Gently heat the cream until warm and of pouring consistency. Keep warm over hot water.

Run a knife round each mousse and turn out on to individual plates or saucers. Spoon some chive cream around each mousse and garnish with a parsley leaf. Serve straight away.

POMMES DE TERRE PERSILLÉES

PARSLEY POTATOES

I am always delighted to discover new recipes for potatoes. One summer, my friend and neighbour in the Ardèche, Madame Marquet, showed me how she prepares this simple dish of potatoes layered with fresh parsley and bay leaves.

SERVES 4

450 g (1 lb) potatoes, peeled
55 g (2 oz) butter
2 fresh bay leaves
3 tablespoons chopped parsley
salt and freshly milled pepper
150 ml (¼ pint) single cream or milk

Slice the potatoes thinly. Butter an ovenproof dish and place a bay leaf on the bottom. Cover with a layer of potatoes and sprinkle with parsley and some salt and pepper. Continue to make layers of potatoes, parsley and seasoning, finishing with a layer of potatoes. Place the other bay leaf on top and dot with the remaining butter. Pour over the cream or milk.

Bake in a moderately hot oven (190°C, 375°F, gas mark 5) for 50–60 minutes until the potatoes are tender.

ARTICHAUTS
À LA BARIGOULE

ARTICHOKES
WITH BACON AND SORREL

There are many versions of this dish – one of the oldest Provençal ways of preparing the delicious globe artichoke. This one comes from a book of old Provençal recipes and varies little from that given in the classic book, *Les Plats Régionaux de France* by Austin de Croze. The best artichokes for this dish are the small purple-leaved variety that are picked from the side shoots of the plants when they are only 4 cm (1½ in) across. At this size the hairy chokes have not formed and the whole artichoke can be eaten.

SERVES 5 – 6

10 – 12 small artichokes
4 tablespoons olive oil
2 medium onions, finely chopped
30 g (1 oz) green bacon, diced
150 ml (¼ pint) water
3 large handfuls of sorrel leaves
salt and freshly milled pepper
300 ml (½ pint) dry white wine
6 new potatoes, diced

Trim the stalks and the tips of any pointed leaves on the artichokes. Wash in cold water and drain well. I usually leave the artichokes whole, but you can quarter them if you prefer.

Heat the oil in a pan and cook the onions until golden and transparent. Add the bacon and cook until the fat runs. Pour in the water and add half the sorrel. Lay the artichokes on top and season lightly with salt and pepper. Cover with the remaining sorrel and add the wine. Cover the pan and cook over low heat for 30 minutes.

Add the potatoes and cook for a further 30 minutes adding a little extra water if necessary. When the dish is cooked the sorrel and the liquid should have cooked down to a smooth sauce.

POIS MANGETOUT
À LA FRANÇAISE

MANGE-TOUT PEAS
WITH LETTUCE AND CHIVES

The delicate flavour of tender mange-tout peas is brought out when they are cooked 'in the French style' with butter, lettuce and chives.

SERVES 3 – 4

225 g (8 oz) mange-tout peas
45 g (1½ oz) butter
a pinch of sugar
salt
½ small cabbage lettuce, shredded
1 tablespoon finely chopped chives
2 finely sliced spring onions
GARNISH
a handful of mint leaves

Trim the ends from the mange-tout. Melt all but a large knob of the butter in a pan and stir in the mange-tout. Add the sugar and salt, cover the pan and cook over moderate heat for 5 minutes.

Stir in the lettuce, chives and spring onion, gently tossing the vegetables together until the lettuce has wilted.

Add the remaining butter and when it has melted serve the vegetables straight away, with a garnish of mint leaves.

POIS MANGETOUT À LA FRANÇAISE *top*, LA CRIQUE *below (p. 130)*.

LA CRIQUE

La crique is a classic potato dish from the Ardèche – a variation on a type of coarse potato pancake that is to be found all over Europe. It usually accompanies roast or grilled meat, but when times are hard, the dish is served on its own. There are several versions; some are so plain they do not even include garlic or herbs in the recipe; others are very rich with the addition of eggs and *crème fraîche*. But this recipe with garlic and parsley seems to be the most popular.

SERVES 3 – 4

450 g (1 lb) potatoes
1 clove garlic, crushed
1 tablespoon finely chopped parsley
salt
oil for shallow frying

Peel the potatoes and grate them into a bowl. Add the garlic, parsley and salt and mix well.

Heat a little oil in a frying pan until very hot. Put

tablespoons of the mixture in the pan, making three or four flat heaps. Cook until golden brown on both sides. Drain well on kitchen paper and serve straight away.

The alternative method is to pile the mixture into the pan and make one large potato cake, turning it over once. Serve cut into wedges.

HARLEQUIN HERBS *Small cloth sacks, printed in a glorious jumble of different colours, contain dried lavender.*

HARICOTS VERTS EN ROBE ÉCARLATE

FRENCH BEANS IN A SCARLET COAT

Towards the end of the season for French beans I look around for alternative ways of serving them. In this Provençal recipe they are cooked with a thick tomato and herb sauce. The dish is very good eaten hot but I prefer to serve it cold as a salad accompanying a main course or as part of an hors-d'oeuvre.

SERVES 4

450 g (1 lb) slim French beans
2 – 3 tablespoons olive oil
1 medium onion, finely chopped
1 clove garlic, finely chopped
450 g (1 lb) ripe tomatoes, peeled and chopped
a splash of red wine
a little sugar
a few sprigs of parsley
a sprig of thyme
a sprig of basil
1 bay leaf
salt and freshly milled pepper
1 tablespoon chopped basil or parsley

Trim the ends off the French beans. Either leave the beans whole or cut them into short lengths. Cook in boiling salted water for 8 – 10 minutes, then drain. Refresh in cold water and drain well once more.

Heat the oil in a saucepan and cook the onion until golden. Add the garlic, tomatoes, wine, sugar, sprigs of herbs, bay leaf and some salt and pepper. Bring to the boil then cover and cook over low heat for 15 minutes. Add the beans and cook for 20 – 30 minutes over low heat until the sauce is thick.

Turn into a serving dish and discard the sprigs of herbs. Either serve straight away, sprinkled with the chopped basil or parsley, or allow to cool then add the freshly chopped herbs and serve.

CAROTTES À L'ANIS

CARROTS WITH FRESH ANISEED

French cooks customarily serve hot carrots, whole or sliced, with herb butter melting over them. Parsley or chive butter is the usual choice. However, in this recipe the uncommon flavour of fresh aniseed complements the sweet taste of a buttery purée of carrots. If fresh aniseed is not available, add a little dried aniseed and a dash of pastis instead.

COOKING INSTRUCTIONS *Little baskets lined with gaily printed Provençal fabrics hold dried herbs – tarragon, basil, marjoram and oregano at the back; sage, wild thyme, savory, rosemary and garden thyme at the front. Some of the labels suggest culinary uses for the herbs as well as giving the price.*

SERVES 4

450 g (1 lb) carrots, scrubbed or peeled
1 teaspoon sugar
salt
115 g (4 oz) butter
2 teaspoons aniseed leaves, finely chopped, or $\frac{1}{4}$ teaspoon dried aniseed, ground to a powder, and a dash of Pernod or other pastis

Slice the carrots thickly into a pan. Add the sugar and salt and cold water to cover. Bring to the boil, cover and cook for 10–20 minutes or until tender.

Drain and then purée the carrots. Return to the pan, add the butter, aniseed and Pernod if using, and cook gently, stirring all the time, over low heat until the butter has melted and any surplus water has been evaporated from the purée. Spoon the carrot purée into a hot serving dish.

FÈVES
À LA CRÈME DE SARRIETTE

BROAD BEANS
WITH SUMMER SAVORY CREAM

Summer savory, *sarriette*, is a traditional flavouring for broad beans in France, but it has a peppery, slightly bitter taste and it is wise to be cautious with the amount you use at first.

SERVES 3 – 4

340 g (12 oz) young broad beans, shelled
a few sprigs of fresh summer savory
30 g (1 oz) butter
150 ml (¼ pint) crème fraîche or soured cream
1 egg yolk
salt and freshly milled pepper

Steam the broad beans or cook them in boiling salted water with half the savory until tender, then drain and discard the savory.

Melt the butter in a pan and add the beans and the remaining savory, finely chopped. Mix the *crème fraîche* with the egg yolk and add to the pan. Cook, stirring, over moderate heat for a few minutes until the cream thickens. Do not allow the sauce to boil or it will curdle. Season to taste. Turn the beans into a hot dish and serve straight away.

SALADE
DE PÊCHES AU POURPIER

PEACH AND PURSLANE SALAD

Purslane is one of the most neglected culinary herbs, yet only a century ago it was highly popular in French gardens and kitchens. Nineteenth-century French cookery books contain many recipes for purslane. It was often cooked like spinach or prepared as a gratin. In the South of France wild purslane was once so abundant that it was made into soups and automatically added to a mixed green salad.

When I started to grow purslane, I was so delighted with the lovely, slightly hazelnut flavour of the fleshy leaves that I started to use it in different summer salads. This combination of purslane with ripe peaches or nectarines garnished with flaked, toasted hazelnuts has a particularly good flavour.

SERVES 1

hazelnut oil
1 ripe peach or nectarine
a handful of freshly picked purslane leaves
3 or 4 hazelnuts, toasted and sliced
freshly milled coriander seed

Brush a small salad plate with hazelnut oil. Peel the peach but leave the skin on if you are using a nectarine. Slice the fruit finely and arrange on the plate in two rows of a semicircle.

Arrange the leaves of purslane in curved lines to complete the circle of salad. Use the smallest leaves to decorate the spaces between the slices of fruit. Trickle the oil over the salad and sprinkle the hazelnuts over the top. Season lightly with freshly milled coriander seed.

SALADE DE PÊCHES AU POURPIER *overleaf left*, SALADE CHAMPÊTRE *overleaf right (p. 136)*.

SALADE CHAMPÊTRE

COUNTRY SALAD

Traditionally the leaves and flowers for this delightful salad are collected during a country picnic or ramble, consequently there are no hard and fast rules for its composition. The essence is to pick a variety of tiny sprigs of salad leaves and herbs – ideally from the fields and garden. The resulting mixed salad has a charm and intensity of flavour which is unforgettable.

SERVES I

a large handful of tiny sprigs of saladings chosen
from the following leaves and herbs:
*lamb's lettuce (*mâche*), oak leaf lettuce (*feuilles*
de chêne*), fine fronds of endive frisée, salad*
*rocket (*roquette*), floppy-leaved basil, opal,*
basil, chervil, flat-leaf parsley, fennel, feverfew,
borage flowers, clary, heartsease, pansies,
marigolds, mallow flowers, mint, purslane,
lemon balm or melissa, thyme flowers, oregano,
marjoram, caraway, hyssop, tarragon,
lovage, nasturtium flowers, summer savory,
sweet cicely, vervain
a light nut oil – hazelnut or almond
*elderflower vinegar (*page 48*)*

Select a pretty salad plate for each person – in hot weather it is a good idea to chill the plates lightly first. Arrange the leaves, herbs and flowers, taking care not to make the salad too large, and placing the leaves delicately so that their size and shape are seen to advantage. Serve straight away and hand a light nut oil and the elderflower vinegar separately for trickling over the salad just before eating.

SALADE DE POIVRONS AUX PIGNONS ET AU BASILIC

SALAD OF SWEET PEPPERS WITH PINE NUTS AND BASIL

In France, this excellent salad of sweet peppers is usually prepared with red peppers only, but I quite like the garish look of red and yellow peppers together that is reminiscent of a painting by Van Gogh. These days there is a good choice of green, red, yellow, orange and even purple sweet peppers, but I usually select just one or two kinds. On the whole the lighter, brighter colours taste sweeter than the darker ones.

SERVES 4

450 g (1 lb) sweet red and yellow peppers
*2–3 tablespoons basil-flavoured oil (*page 118*)*
2 tablespoons pine nuts
1–2 tablespoons lemon juice
2 teaspoons finely chopped fresh basil
salt

Wash and dry the peppers and place in a flameproof dish under a hot grill, turning them over several times until the skin is cooked, blistered and blackened on all sides.

Remove the dish from the grill and cover with an upturned bowl that seals in the air. For a small number of peppers you can transfer them to a plastic or paper bag, then seal and leave to cool.

Peel the peppers and then cut into strips, discarding all the seeds and the stem. Arrange the peppers on a serving dish or plate.

Heat the oil in a small pan and add the pine nuts. Cook, stirring, until the nuts are just starting to brown. Add the lemon juice to the pan. Spoon the dressing over the peppers and season with a little salt. Garnish with fresh basil and serve when lukewarm or cool.

SALADE DE PISSENLITS AUX LARDONS

DANDELION SALAD WITH BACON

Dandelion leaves, blanched under a flower pot to make them less bitter, taste similar to endive, and this excellent salad can be made equally well with endive instead of dandelions. *Lard fumé* is a fine-flavoured cured, smoked belly pork. If you cannot find it, use smoked streaky bacon instead for this recipe.

SERVES 4

225 g (8 oz) blanched dandelion leaves or endive
1 – 2 cloves garlic, according to taste
½ teaspoon Dijon mustard
1 tablespoon wine vinegar
salt and freshly milled pepper
2 tablespoons olive oil
2 tablespoons sunflower oil
½ ficelle or ¼ baguette loaf, sliced thinly
150 g (5 oz) lard fumé or smoked streaky bacon, diced

Wash the dandelion leaves or endive in plenty of cold water and shake dry in a salad basket.

Crush the garlic in the bottom of your salad bowl (I prefer to use a wooden one for this salad) and blend with the mustard and half the wine vinegar. Season with salt and pepper and gradually blend in the olive oil to make the dressing. Toss the dandelion leaves with the dressing until they are well coated.

Heat the remaining olive oil with the sunflower oil and fry the slices of bread until crisp and golden to make *croûtons*. True garlic lovers rub the hot *croûtons* with a clove of garlic before adding them to the salad.

Now fry the *lard fumé* or bacon until crisp to make lardons and toss them over the salad. Pour the remaining vinegar into the pan, swirl to incorporate with the bacon fat and pour over the salad. Serve straight away.

SALADE DE MESCLUN À L'HUILE DE NOISETTE

MESCLUN SALAD WITH HAZELNUT OIL

Mesclun is the Provençal name for a mixture of small salad leaves. It usually comprises *endive frisée*, red radicchio, *scarole*, lamb's lettuce (*mâche*), oak leaf lettuce (*feuilles de chêne*), small leaves of cos lettuce (*laitue romaine*), and some sprigs of herbs such as chervil, flat-leaf parsley and salad rocket (*roquette*).

In recent years this idea has become popular with gardeners in northern Europe who grow several varieties of salading together. These are then cropped by cutting only a few leaves at a time, thereby allowing the plants to grow a further crop. This salad mixture is sometimes described in seed catalogues as a 'cut-and-come-again' crop.

Hazelnut oil, *huile de noisette*, has a lovely distinctive flavour and is well worth hunting for, but if it is unavailable you can use olive oil instead.

SERVES 4

200 g (7 oz) mesclun or mixed small salad leaves
a small paring of garlic, crushed
⅛ teaspoon Dijon mustard
3 – 4 tablespoons hazelnut oil
2 – 3 teaspoons white wine vinegar, preferably d'Orleans
salt and freshly milled mignonnette pepper (page 96)

Wash the salad leaves carefully and dry well in a salad basket.

In a salad bowl mix the garlic with the mustard and blend in the oil and the vinegar. Season with salt and freshly milled mignonnette pepper.

Add the salad leaves and toss until coated with the dressing. Serve straight away.

DESSERTS, CAKES AND PRESERVES

Scented herbs impart their perfume to many of the desserts and pastries for which French cooks are so famous, as well as flavouring pickles, preserves, liqueurs and tisanes.

TARTE AUX PÊCHES À L'HYSOPE *left (p. 142)*, MELON
FARCI AUX FRUITS ET AUX FLEURS *centre (p. 144)*,
QUATRE-QUARTS AU GERANIUM ROSE *right (p. 152)*.

Every summer, on my last morning in the Ardèche, my friend and neighbour, Madame Marquet, pays me a visit. For once, she is empty handed and is not bringing freshly picked produce from her garden. She knows that today I must clean the house and pack the car, and there's scarcely time enough to eat, let alone cook. We both feel sad. Apart from exchanging New Year cards, we shall not be in touch until the spring, when I telephone to say that I am returning.

She fusses over me, making sure that I've done this and not forgotten that. 'And remember,' she says, 'to go and pick the lavender – as much as you can carry.' And we part, until later that day, when I shall call on her to say goodbye properly.

After I've swept and washed the house, and forbidden anyone to enter, I slowly make my way out into the Marquets' lavender fields. I look at the sky, cloudless and very bright blue above the sea of purple, then my gaze follows the outline of the surrounding hills, ancient, dark and slightly hazy in the heat. I glance back at the hamlet that I feel part of, and finally, I bend down and start to pick the lavender.

Preserving herbs for sweet dishes is delightfully easy. I recommend making several herb-scented sugars and honeys. The sugars are excellent sprinkled on custards, shortbreads and sponge cakes, or they can be used for sweetening and flavouring the mixture when making cakes, biscuits and puddings. Herb-scented honey can replace ordinary honey as a sweetener and it is also very good spread on fresh bread or hot toast.

For the best results, choose herbs that are dry and pick them towards mid-day when their aromatic oils are warm and scented. The herbs most suitable for scenting sugar and honey are angelica, aniseed, bay, rose geranium, hyssop, lavender, lemon balm, marigold flowers, mint (especially eau-de-cologne mint, pine-apple mint and peppermint), rosemary, sweet cicely, verbena, vervain, violet.

HERB-SCENTED SUGARS

To make lavender sugar, mix 55 g (2 oz) of spikes of fresh lavender flowers (with the stalks cut off if necessary), or 30 g (1 oz) of dried lavender flowers, with 225 g (8 oz) of caster sugar.

Select a dry glass jar and make alternate layers of sugar and lavender flowers until the jar is full. Cover tightly and leave in a warm room for 1–2 weeks. Give the jar an occasional shake to distribute the scent evenly. Shake the sugar through a nylon sieve before use. Return the lavender flowers to the jar and top up with fresh sugar.

Rose-petal sugar is a lovely preparation. Select the petals from well-scented roses – on the whole, deep-red roses have the most perfume. Make as for lavender sugar and use within 4–6 weeks while the flavour of the lavender is still strong.

Vanilla sugar is made in the same way as other scented sugars. Bury a vanilla pod, broken in two, in a jar of caster sugar. Top up the jar with fresh sugar as you use it.

HERB-SCENTED HONEY

I find that clear liquid honey works best and absorbs the scent from the herb more readily than set honey. Liquid honey can be turned into set honey by chilling, and, of course, set honey can be liquified by leaving the jar in a warm place or in the sun for a few days.

To make rosemary-scented honey, slightly warm a 500 g (1 lb) jar of clear honey by leaving the jar in a warm place for 24 hours. Add 4 sprigs of rosemary (preferably flowering) to the honey, screw on the cap tightly and leave in a warm room for 1–2 weeks. Now and again, turn the jar over to distribute the scent evenly. I usually leave the herb in the jar since it looks attractive.

CRÈME ANGLAISE
AUX FEUILLES DE PÊCHER

PEACH LEAF CUSTARD

French cooks have always been noted for their resourcefulness. Not only do they cook with a wide range of culinary herbs, but they also use unusual leaves and flowers to flavour foods. In this recipe peach leaves are used to give a delicate custard a gentle, almond-like taste. A fig leaf also imparts a unique flavour.

SERVES 4 – 6

500 ml (18 fl oz) milk
6 fresh peach leaves
5 egg yolks
100 g (3½ oz) sugar
FOR SERVING
langue de chat biscuits or almond tuile biscuits

Heat the milk with the peach leaves to just under boiling point. Remove from the heat and set aside to infuse for 5 minutes.

Whisk the egg yolks with the sugar. Strain on the milk, whisking all the time. Return the mixture to the pan, preferably a double boiler, and cook gently, stirring, until slightly thickened. Do not let the mixture boil or the custard will be spoiled. Remove from the heat then stand the pan in cold water to cool it.

Pour the custard into small glasses and leave until cold. Serve with langue de chat or almond tuile biscuits, or fingers of hot toasted brioche.

BUSHELS OF LAVENDER *Villagers in the South of France with only a field or two of lavender gather it and take the bundles to a central distillery to be made into an oil which they then sell. The pungent oil is a powerful antiseptic.*

TARTE AUX PÊCHES À L'HYSOPE

PEACH TART WITH HYSSOP

'Purge him with hyssop' it says in the Bible. Despite this advice the pink or, more commonly, blue-flowered herb is worth growing to attract bees and to be able to revive the very old combination of peaches with hyssop.

SERVES 6

PASTRY

115 g (4 oz) plain flour

30 g (1 oz) plus $\frac{1}{2}$ teaspoon caster sugar

45 g (1$\frac{1}{2}$ oz) finely ground, unblanched hazelnuts

75 g (2$\frac{1}{2}$ oz) butter, half-frozen

1 egg, separated

1 tablespoon milk

a few drops of vanilla essence

FILLING

6 medium-sized fresh peaches

115 g (4 oz) granulated sugar

150 ml ($\frac{1}{4}$ pint) water

4 sprigs of hyssop

1 teaspoon arrowroot

TO GARNISH

a few leaves of hyssop and some hyssop flowers, if available

Sieve the flour and 30 g (1 oz) caster sugar into a bowl, then stir in the hazelnuts. Grate in the butter and mix to a dough with the egg yolk, milk and vanilla essence. Roll the dough into a ball and rest under the upturned bowl for 15 minutes.

On a floured board, roll out the pastry to line a greased 22 cm (8$\frac{1}{2}$ in) tart tin. Prick the base of the pastry lightly and bake the pastry case blind in a moderate oven (180°C, 350°F, gas mark 4) for 15 minutes until it is just changing colour at the edges. Lightly whisk the egg white with the $\frac{1}{2}$ teaspoon of caster sugar and brush over the inside of the pastry case. Return to the oven for 5 minutes until the

pastry is golden brown and the egg white has cooked to a glaze. Cool the pastry case in the tin.

Cover the peaches with boiling water for a few minutes then lift out and skin. Slice the fruit.

Dissolve the sugar in the water over moderate heat then simmer with three sprigs of the hyssop for 4 minutes. Remove the sprigs of hyssop and add the peaches. Poach gently for 4–5 minutes until the fruit is tender but not overcooked. Lift it out with a slotted spoon and add the arrowroot, mixed with a little water, to the pan. Cook, stirring, until clear and thickened.

Remove from the heat, stir in the chopped leaves of the remaining sprig of hyssop and cool slightly. Arrange the peach slices in overlapping circles in the tart case and spoon the syrup over the fruit. Decorate with the extra leaves and flowers. Serve at room temperature within 2 hours while the pastry is still crisp.

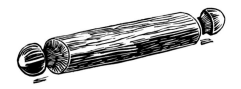

TARTE À LA FRANGIPANE ET AUX VIOLETTES

FRANGIPANE TART WITH CRYSTALLIZED VIOLETS

I have spent many hours gazing at the wondrous confections displayed in the windows of French *pâtisseries*. Sometimes, to the interest of passers-by, I sketch what I see. Eventually, unable to wait any longer, I enter and buy at least one of the cakes that have fascinated me.

In England I make this frangipane tart to bring back a memory or two of all those happy cake hours that I have spent in France. I usually decorate the tart with crystallized violets but many other small spring flowers can be candied and used for decorating puddings, tarts and cakes. Try the same method with primroses, rosemary or borage flowers and polyanthus blooms.

SERVES 6

180 g (6 oz) prepared-weight shortcrust or flaky pastry

30 g (1 oz) icing sugar

warm water

a few drops of orange flower water

FRANGIPANE CREAM

115 g (4 oz) butter

115 g (4 oz) vanilla-flavoured caster sugar (page 140)

2 eggs

115 g (4 oz) ground almonds

30 g (1 oz) plain flour

1 – 2 teaspoons orange flower water or to taste

CRYSTALLIZED VIOLETS

a handful of fresh violets

1 egg white

caster sugar

Make the frangipane cream by creaming the butter with the sugar until light and fluffy. Beat in the eggs one at a time and then work in the ground almonds and the flour. Add orange flower water to taste.

Roll out the pastry to fit a 20 cm (7 – 8 in) tart tin. Brush inside the pastry case with some of the lightly beaten egg white and then spoon in the frangipane cream, smoothing it level. Bake on a hot baking sheet in a hot oven (200°C, 400°F, gas mark 6) for 30 – 35 minutes until golden brown. Cool in the tin.

While the tart is still warm, make the icing by mixing the sieved icing sugar with enough warm water to make a pouring consistency. Flavour to taste with orange flower water. Trickle the icing over the top of the tart and put aside to set.

Make the crystallized violets by brushing the petals of the fresh flowers on both sides with lightly beaten egg white. Dust lightly with caster sugar all over and leave to dry on a sheet of greaseproof paper in a warm place. Decorate the tart by arranging the violets in a ring on top.

PETITS COEURS DE CRÈME AUX FRAISES DES BOIS ET AUX FLEURS DE SUREAU

LITTLE HEART-SHAPED CREAMS WITH WILD STRAWBERRIES AND ELDERFLOWERS

Traditionally, these little drained cream cheeses from the Loire valley are made in early summer with thick, rich cream. A few sweet, wild strawberries, *fraises des bois*, are strewn on top. I like to pour a little muscat-scented syrup made from elderflowers around the creams.

SERVES 4

300 ml (½ pint) double cream

2 egg whites

MUSCAT SYRUP

115 g (4 oz) green gooseberries

115 g (4 oz) caster sugar

2 tablespoons water

2 heads of elderflower blossom

FOR SERVING

about 24 whole wild strawberries, or some sliced cultivated strawberries

Beat the cream until thick but still glossy. Whisk the egg whites until stiff. Fold the egg whites into the cream and spoon the mixture into four heart-shaped china moulds lined with damp muslin. Leave in a cold place overnight to drain.

To make the muscat-scented syrup, cook the gooseberries (don't bother to top and tail them) with the sugar and water over low heat until soft. Remove the gooseberries from the heat, add the elderflowers and leave for 3 minutes to infuse. Strain the syrup from the fruit and flowers into a small jug and set aside to cool.

The next day unmould each cream on to a small plate. Decorate with the wild strawberries and pour over some of the elderflower syrup.

MELON FARCI AUX FRUITS ET AUX FLEURS

MELON STUFFED WITH FRUIT AND FLOWERS

The idea for this dish came from a highly innovative French cookery book, *Plats nouveaux! essai de gastronomie moderne*, written by Paul Reboux in 1927. At the time the book was banned in America because some of the recipes were regarded as unsuitable. Thirty years later an English translation was published, entitled *Food for the Rich*. Fortunately, though, you don't have to be rich to try this charming and delicious idea.

SERVES 4

4 small, ripe charentais melons

a few other fresh seasonal fruits such as raspberries, strawberries, peaches, black currants, figs and stoned cherries

85 – 115 g (3 – 4 oz) caster sugar

4 tablespoons fruit liqueur, Muscat wine or champagne

a handful of edible herb flowers such as nasturtiums, rosemary, marigold petals, sage, or rose petals

about 24 nasturtium flowers with stems

Wipe the melons with a damp cloth. Use a sharp knife to cut across the top of each melon to make a round opening large enough to take a tablespoon. Scoop out the seeds and discard. Scoop the flesh into a bowl, either using a melon baller or a teaspoon, taking care not to puncture the skin.

Add a selection of the summer fruits, diced or sliced as appropriate, to the melon flesh and mix in the sugar. Pour the wine over the fruit and leave covered in a cold place for at least 30 minutes.

Sprinkle the flower petals over the fruit and spoon it into the melon shells. Arrange some nasturtium flowers in the opening to conceal the fruit. In hot weather serve the melons standing on beds of chipped ice in shallow bowls.

OEUFS À LA NEIGE AUX ROSES

SNOW EGGS WITH ROSE PETALS

A specially fine summer day in my English garden inspired this version of the classic French pudding that is always popular with children. Pink or red rose petals are usually the most highly scented and are the best for crystallizing. The scented sugar needs to be made a few hours ahead.

SERVES 6

ROSE-SCENTED SUGAR

a handful of scented rose petals

100 g (3½ oz) caster sugar

OEUFS À LA NEIGE

570 ml (1 pint) milk

3 eggs, separated

1 teaspoon rose water

1 – 2 tablespoons raspberry purée or 1 – 2 drops of pink vegetable food colouring

CRYSTALLIZED ROSE PETALS

12 pink rose petals

1 egg white, lightly whisked

Layer the rose petals with the caster sugar in a jar. Cover with a tight-fitting lid and leave in a warm place for at least 3 – 4 hours until the sugar has taken on the scent of the roses.

Heat the milk in your widest pan over moderate heat. Whisk the egg whites until stiff and fold in 15 g (½ oz) of the scented sugar. Just as the milk comes to the boil, put rounded dessertspoons of the meringue mixture in the milk and poach them, spooning the hot milk over the egg-shaped meringues until they are cooked. This usually takes under a minute. Use a slotted spoon to lift out each snow egg and place in a large shallow serving dish. Repeat until all the meringue has been poached.

Whisk 55 g (2 oz) of the rose-scented sugar with the egg yolks. Pour on the hot milk from the pan. Strain the mixture back into the pan, add any milk that has drained from the snow eggs and cook, stirring, until slightly thickened, never allowing the custard to boil. Stir in the rose water and just enough raspberry purée and or food colouring to make the custard pale pink, ideally a shade to match or complement your rose petals.

Cool the custard and then gently pour it into the serving dish so that the snow eggs float.

Crystallize the rose petals by brushing both sides of a petal with egg white. Sprinkle with some of the remaining scented sugar and place on a sheet of paper in a warm place. Scatter the crystallized petals over the top of the snow eggs and serve.

GRATIN DES FRUITS À L'ANGÉLIQUE

FRUIT GRATIN WITH ANGELICA

Both angelica and sweet cicely have the useful characteristic of making sharp or acid fruit taste sweeter. In this dish I use angelica leaves to 'sweeten' the fruit and have added candied or crystallized stems of the herb to the covering of cream. This fruit gratin can be prepared with whatever soft fruits are in season.

SERVES 4

2 large peaches, peeled and sliced
a few strawberries
a few raspberries
a handful of red currants and black currants
1 young leaf of angelica, chopped
2 tablespoons kirsch or Grand Marnier (optional)
100 g ($3\frac{1}{2}$ oz) caster sugar
300 ml ($\frac{1}{2}$ pint) double cream
20 g ($\frac{3}{4}$ oz) crystallized angelica, finely chopped

Divide the fruit between four small gratin dishes. You can use one large dish, but I think individual servings are more attractive. Add the chopped angelica leaf to the fruit and sprinkle over the liqueur, if you are using it, and half the sugar.

Beat the cream until stiff but still glossy, mix in the crystallized angelica and spread over the fruit. Smooth the surface and chill for at least 30 minutes.

Sprinkle the remaining sugar in an even layer over the cream and place the dishes under a hot grill for 6–8 minutes until the sugar has melted and caramelized. Allow the dishes to cool and then chill until ready to serve.

TRADITIONAL HERBALISM *A trained herbalist in an old Paris shop carefully weighs out rose petals, purple mallow flowers, marigold petals and chamomile flowers.*

OEUFS À LA NEIGE AUX ROSES *overleaf.*

145

CRÊPES DE BLÉ NOIR AUX FRAISES CHAUDES ET MENTHÉES

BUCKWHEAT CRÊPES WITH HOT MINTED STRAWBERRIES

Buckwheat crêpes are a speciality of Normandy. I like to fill them with hot strawberries cooked in a mint-flavoured syrup and topped with cool *crème fraîche*.

SERVES 4–6

CRÊPE BATTER
1 large egg
150 ml ($\frac{1}{4}$ pint) milk
30 g (1 oz) buckwheat flour
30 g (1 oz) plain flour
30 g (1 oz) butter
FILLING
450 g (1 lb) strawberries
85–115 g (3–4 oz) sugar
1 teaspoon finely chopped mint leaves
150 ml ($\frac{1}{4}$ pint) crème fraîche or soured cream
1 tablespoon icing sugar

Whisk the egg with the milk and gradually beat in the flours. Melt the butter in a 15 cm (6 in) crêpe pan and then mix it into the batter but leave a thin film of butter behind in the pan.

Pour about 2 tablespoons of the batter into the pan and run it across the base to spread it evenly. Cook the crêpe until golden brown on both sides, remove from the pan and keep warm. Make 6 crêpes in all and store them on a warm plate covered with a cloth.

Hull the strawberries, rinse and slice into a pan. Stir in the sugar and mint and cook over moderate heat, stirring, for 3–4 minutes until syrupy.

Lay a crêpe on a warm plate and spoon some strawberries on to one half. Add some *crème fraîche* and then fold over the other half of the crêpe and dust with sieved icing sugar. Serve straight away.

MOUSSE AU CHOCOLAT ET AU MENTHE

CHOCOLATE MOUSSE WITH MINT

Once upon a time the French would have regarded this combination of flavours with horror. However, during the last decade, *nouvelle cuisine* has introduced many new ideas to French cooking and although not all of them have survived, a chocolate mousse spiked with fresh mint has remained popular.

SERVES 4–6

100 g ($3\frac{1}{2}$ oz) plain dessert chocolate
3 tablespoons black coffee
1 tablespoon kirsch
1 teaspoon finely chopped mint
4 eggs, separated
4–6 leaves or sprigs of mint for decoration

Melt the chocolate with the coffee and the kirsch in a pan over low heat, stirring gently now and again until the mixture is smooth. Remove from the heat and mix in the chopped mint and the egg yolks, one at a time.

Whisk the egg whites until stiff. Gradually fold the chocolate mixture into the egg whites, taking care not to lose too much air. Spoon the mousse into 4–6 small dishes or pots and leave in a cool place to set.

Just before serving, decorate each mousse with the extra mint leaves.

BEIGNETS DE FEUILLES DE BOURRACHE DE PAUL REBOUX

PAUL REBOUX'S BORAGE FRITTERS

Some years ago, I was given a collection of French cookery books by a dear couple that I met by chance in a quiet street in Hyères on the Mediterranean coast. Among the books was a yellowed copy dating from 1927 of *Plats Nouveaux* by Paul Reboux whose recipes are deliciously unusual.

Borage fritters are an old Burgundian delicacy. Reboux includes this recipe: 'Steep the leaves in brandy for an hour and drain them well. Fill each with a little frangipane cream and roll them up. Dip in batter and fry.' This is how I make these lovely little morsels.

SERVES 4–6

about 24 young borage leaves
2–3 tablespoons brandy or eau-de-vie
frangipane cream (page 143)
BATTER
55 g (2 oz) plain flour, sieved
a pinch of salt
60 ml (2 fl oz) warm water
1 tablespoon sunflower oil
1 egg white
sunflower oil for deep-frying
a little extra vanilla-flavoured sugar (page 140)

Remove the stems from the borage leaves and arrange the leaves in a shallow dish. Pour over the brandy or *eau-de-vie* and leave in a warm place for 1 hour. Meanwhile make the frangipane cream.

Strain the brandy from the borage leaves into a bowl. Set aside the leaves. Make the batter by whisking the sieved flour and salt with the water and the oil until smooth. Beat in the brandy. Whisk the egg white until stiff and fold into the batter.

Drain the borage leaves well and place a spoonful of frangipane cream towards the stalk end of each leaf and roll up. Dip in the batter and deep-fry in very hot sunflower oil (180°C, 355°F) for 3–4 minutes until golden. Drain on kitchen paper, then dust with vanilla sugar and serve.

GELÉE DE LA LAVANDE

LAVENDER JELLY

I have discovered that when warm dessert wine is poured on to fresh lavender flowers, a pinky-red infusion results that, sweetened, has an intriguing and attractive flavour. With the addition of a little orange juice and gelatine it sets into a delightful jelly.

SERVES 4

55 g (2 oz) fresh lavender flowers, or 30 g (1 oz) dried lavender flowers
425 ml (¾ pint) Montbazillac white dessert wine
30–55 g (1–2 oz) lavender sugar (page 140) or according to taste
1 sachet (11 g, .4 oz) powdered gelatine
juice of 1 orange

Put the lavender flowers into a glass or enamel pan (not a metal one) and add the wine. Heat very gently until the temperature reaches blood heat (37°C, 98°F). Remove from the heat and set aside for 10 minutes to infuse.

Strain the wine into a bowl, pressing on the flowers with the back of a spoon to extract all the flavour. Stir the sugar into the wine until dissolved. Check the flavour and add sugar if necessary.

Sprinkle the gelatine into the orange juice and leave to soften, then warm gently until dissolved. Stir into the wine mixture and pour the jelly into a pretty glass dish or into four stemmed glasses. Chill the jelly until set.

Let the jelly almost reach room temperature before serving so that it is nicely wobbly and the flavour is at its best.

GLACE DE LA LAVANDE

LAVENDER ICE CREAM

Until I started to write this book I had conducted few culinary experiments with lavender. I decided, though, that by the time I arrived at the final chapter this would be my lavender summer.

It was July, and my own English lavender, like a gentle echo of that in the fields of Provence, was covered with the long mauve spikes of scented flowers. Before long the bushes were shorn and I carried every bloom into the kitchen. The house began to smell wonderful – everywhere you walked the small grey seeds gave off their beautiful scent. I discovered that even the leaves of lavender can give a lovely flavour in cooking. Now there are just a few flowers left. Just enough to keep by the fire for throwing on to the flames during the winter, to produce that hazy softly-scented smoke that reminds one of summer.

SERVES 6 – 8

2 tablespoons finely chopped fresh lavender leaves
2 tablespoons white dessert wine such as a
Muscat, a Sauternes or a Montbazillac
500 ml (18 fl oz) double cream
100 g (3½ oz) lavender sugar (page 140)
2 egg whites
2 tablespoons fresh lavender flowers

Stir the lavender leaves into the wine and leave in a warm place for 10 minutes to infuse. Beat the cream until stiff but still glossy and gradually mix in the strained wine with half the sugar.

Whisk the egg whites until stiff then whisk in the remaining sugar. Fold the egg whites into the cream with the lavender flowers.

Spoon the mixture into a bowl or box and freeze.

GELÉE DE LA LAVANDE *(p. 149)*, GLACE DE LA LAVANDE, BATONNETS AU VIN DOUX ET À LA LAVANDE.

BATONNETS AU VIN DOUX ET À LA LAVANDE

SWEET WINE LAVENDER BISCUITS

A friend who lives near Beaumes-de-Venise in Vaucluse gave me the basic recipe for these biscuits – I added the lavender. She uses the lovely Muscat wine made in the village which gives the biscuits a delightful flavour. Sometimes, for a change, I make the biscuits with Montbazillac, a dessert wine from the Dordogne, and it works just as well.

I serve these biscuits with Lavender Jelly or Lavender Ice Cream. They are also nice served on their own with a glass of dessert wine – in France, in the summer, we often slice a peach into our wine and then eat the fruit with the biscuits and finally drink the wine.

MAKES ABOUT 30 BISCUITS

130 g (4½ oz) plain flour
85 g (3 oz) lavender sugar (page 140)
a pinch of salt
55 g (2 oz) butter
2 – 2½ tablespoons sweet white wine (see above)
12 leaves of fresh lavender, finely chopped

Sieve the flour, all but 1 tablespoon of the sugar, and the salt into a bowl. Rub in the butter until the mixture resembles breadcrumbs. Make a well in the centre and add the wine and the lavender leaves and stir in gently. Leave the mixture for 10 minutes, stirring now and again, by which time it will have bonded together, then gather together to make a soft dough.

Roll out the dough on a floured board to about 3 mm (⅛ in) thick and use a serrated pasta wheel to cut out strips about 6 × 2.5 cm (2½ × 1 in). Place on a buttered baking tray, giving one half of each strip a twist as you do so to make the biscuits look like bows. Bake in a moderately hot oven (190°C, 375°F, gas mark 5) for 6 – 8 minutes or until the edges are just turning brown. Cool on a wire rack and sprinkle with the remaining sugar.

BISCUITS AU ROMARIN

ROSEMARY SHORTBREAD BISCUITS

My French friends are always intrigued and delighted by home-made English biscuits and Dundee Cake. One year Madame Marquet asked me to show her how to make them. Whenever possible, I travel south carrying a supply of both these items plus a few bottles of 'le whisky'. These rosemary biscuits can be eaten on their own and they also make excellent accompaniment to summer ices and fools.

MAKES ABOUT 30 BISCUITS

115 g (4 oz) butter
55 g (2 oz) caster sugar
180 g (6 oz) plain flour
1−2 tablespoons fresh rosemary, finely chopped
a little extra sugar

Cream the butter with the sugar until smooth. Work in the flour and the rosemary to make a soft dough then shape into a ball.

Roll out the dough on a floured board until 0.5 cm ($\frac{1}{4}$ in) thick and cut out rounds using a 5 cm (2 in) fluted cutter.

Bake on a greased baking sheet in a warm oven (160°C, 325°F, gas mark 3) for 15−20 minutes or until the shortbread biscuits are just changing colour. Cool the biscuits on a wire rack and then dust with the extra sugar.

QUATRE-QUARTS AU GERANIUM ROSE

SPONGE CAKE WITH ROSE-SCENTED GERANIUM LEAF

A *quartre-quarts* cake is the French equivalent of an English pound cake in which the ingredients all have the same weight. The pretty leaves of a rose geranium are so strongly scented that two or three placed in the base of the cake tin will perfume the whole cake beautifully. A fluted tin makes the cake look particularly attractive.

MAKES ONE 19 CM ($7\frac{1}{2}$ in) CAKE

2 large eggs
the weight of the unshelled eggs in:
butter
vanilla-flavoured caster sugar (page 140)
plain flour, sieved
1 teaspoon rose water
4 or 5 leaves of rose geranium
a little icing sugar

Cream the butter with the sugar and the rose water until light and fluffy. Beat in the eggs one at a time making sure that the mixture does not separate. Fold in the sieved flour.

Butter a 19 cm ($7\frac{1}{2}$ in) cake tin and then line the base with a circle of buttered greaseproof paper. Sprinkle a thin layer of caster sugar over the inside of the cake tin. Lay the leaves upside down in the base of the tin. Spoon the mixture on top, taking care not to dislodge the leaves.

Bake the cake in a moderate oven, (180°C, 350°F, gas mark 4) for 25−35 minutes or until cooked and springy in the middle. Take care not to overcook the cake. Remove from the oven and cool in the tin for 3 minutes then turn out on to a wire rack. Dust a little sieved icing sugar around the edge of the cake. Serve when cool.

FOUGASSE AU BEURRE ET À L'ANIS

BUTTER FOUGASSE WITH GREEN ANISEED

A *fougasse* is one of the most distinctive breads in France. I have found these loaves all over the south, but there seem to be more variations on the basic simple loaf in Provence. Lionel Poilane, the Parisian baker, thinks that the loaves were originally designed to test the temperature of the bread oven.

In Provence the dough is usually flavoured with salt and olive oil, or it may be kneaded with butter and herbs or spices. This latter kind, as in the recipe that follows, is a special loaf made for festivals and feast days.

MAKES I LOAF

20 g ($\frac{3}{4}$ oz) fresh yeast
2 tablespoons warm water
570 g (1 $\frac{1}{4}$ lb) strong white flour
a pinch of salt
45 g (1 $\frac{1}{2}$ oz) caster sugar
300 ml ($\frac{1}{2}$ pint) milk
200 g (7 oz) butter, softened
2 eggs
20 g ($\frac{3}{4}$ oz) green aniseed, or dried aniseed
beaten egg for glazing
TO DECORATE
1 tablespoon clear honey
diced candied fruit such as cherries and candied angelica

Blend the yeast in a bowl with the warm water and mix in 55 g (2 oz) of the flour. Shape the mixture into a ball, place in the bowl covered with a plastic bag and leave at room temperature for 3 hours.

Sieve the remaining flour on to a work surface or into a wide shallow mixing bowl. Make a well in the middle and add the salt, sugar, milk, and the yeast mixture. Mix well and gradually mix in the butter, the eggs and the green or dried aniseed until

the mixture has formed a smooth dough.

Knead for 3 minutes then roll the dough into a ball and place in a lightly buttered bowl. Cover with a lid or a plastic bag and leave at room temperature for 3 hours.

Turn the dough on to a floured surface and press or roll it into a circle about 25 cm (10 in) across. Place on a floured baking sheet and cut into the circle to make spokes as on a wheel. Brush with beaten egg and set aside in a warm place until the dough is puffy. Bake in a hot oven (200°C, 400°F, gas mark 6) for about 30 minutes. Transfer to a wire rack, brush with honey and decorate with the candied fruit and angelica. Allow to cool.

LA SAUGE MIRACLE

MIRACULOUS SAGE LIQUEUR

I discovered this recipe in a cookery book from Nyons in northern Provence. The author, Mireille Lesbros, says that her grandmother used to make this sage-flavoured liqueur. Interestingly, this is one of the few recipes that I have come across that includes the beautiful blue sage flowers as well as the aromatic leaves.

MAKES 2 litres (3 $\frac{1}{2}$ pints)

a good handful of leaves and flowers of sage
1 litre (1 $\frac{3}{4}$ pints) eau-de-vie, *50° strength*
400 g (14 oz) sugar
500 ml (18 fl oz) water

Place the sage leaves and flowers in a wide-necked bottle or jar and add the *eau-de-vie*. Cover and leave in a warm place for eight days then strain into a bottle. Dissolve the sugar in the water over low heat, then bring to the boil. Cool the syrup and add to the *eau-de-vie*.

Seal the bottle and store in a cool, dark place, or drink immediately. Serve in a small glass as an appetizer or digestive. 'This liqueur can save life!' says Madame Lesbros.

TISANES AUX HERBES

HERB TISANES

When, towards the close of the last century, Marcel Proust tasted that famous madeleine cake dipped in lime tea, he began a momentous journey into his memory which resulted in the magnificent *À la Recherche du Temps Perdu*, and we became the richer.

Although the French have a well-justified reputation as a nation of coffee drinkers, increasingly, the young and those who dine late prefer to drink a tisane – herb tea. Mint tea, for example, taken hot after a meal acts as a digestive, or, when served iced in a long-stemmed glass, is a delightfully cooling concoction on a hot afternoon.

The herbs recommended for making tisanes are angelica, chamomile, catmint, dill, fennel, rose geranium, hyssop, lavender, lemon balm (melissa), lime flowers, marigold, mint (especially apple, eau-de-cologne, ginger and pineapple varieties), rose hip, rosemary, sage, sweet cicely, verbena, vervain, violet.

The recipe below is for *tisane au menthe* (mint tea), but the same method is used for other herbs.

MAKES ABOUT 6 CUPS

4 sprigs of fresh mint or 2 teaspoons dried mint leaves
1 litre (1¾ pints) boiling water
sugar, if desired

Put the fresh or dried mint in a heatproof jug or a very clean teapot. Pour on the boiling water, stir and allow to infuse for 3–5 minutes. Strain into cups or heatproof glasses and serve. Sweeten to taste with sugar.

When I am making a tisane for one person I put the sprig of fresh mint in the cup and pour over the boiling water. Allow to infuse, remove the herb and serve.

To make iced mint tea, make as above then chill. Serve in a stemmed glass with ice cubes and a slice of lemon. Decorate each glass with a tiny sprig of fresh mint or frost the rim with sugar.

VIN D'ORANGES

ORANGE WINE

I add a little fresh angelica to give extra interest to this Burgundian recipe for making an orange-flavoured wine. The wine is sweet enough to accompany a plate of *petits fours* at the end of a meal or try serving it with ice and mineral water to make a refreshing spritzer.

MAKES 1 litre (1¾ pints)

2 large oranges, washed and dried
400 g (14 oz) cube sugar
15 cm (6 in) piece of fresh angelica stalk, cut into short lengths
1 litre (1¾ pints) dry white wine

Use a sharp knife to remove the thin outside zest of the oranges which contains the aromatic oils and flavour. Take care not to include any of the white pith layer under the skin of the orange. Put the orange zest in a bottle or jar with a screw-top. Add the sugar, angelica and the wine. Seal the bottle and leave in a warm place in the kitchen for 14 days, making sure that once a day during this time you briefly shake the bottle.

Strain the wine into a fresh bottle or bottles. Cork and store in a cold dark place until required. The flavour improves with keeping.

SOOTHING FLOWERS *In midsummer, avenues of lime trees are covered with clusters of scented flowers that attract the bees from miles around. The flowers are picked, dried and then used to make a tisane which relaxes and calms the nerves.*

CORNICHONS CONSERVÉS À L'ANETH

PICKLED CUCUMBERS WITH DILL

My mother is Canadian and I was brought up with dill pickles, as these pickled cucumbers are known throughout North America. In July, each summer of my childhood, a day or two – it seemed like a week – was devoted to the business of putting up the pickles. In France you see the small dark green gherkin-cucumbers on sale in the markets from the end of June until September. The vegetable is prepared in the same way as for dill pickles but on the whole the French prefer to flavour the pickling brine with tarragon and garlic rather than dill. In my view both kinds are equally good. If you are buying the gherkins in France, look for the varieties *vert petit de Paris* or *améliore de Bourbonne*.

It is a good idea to use only glass, enamel or wood utensils and tools when preparing these pickles – metal can impair their flavour.

MAKES ABOUT I kg (2¼ lb)

1 kg (2¼ lb) small, firm gherkin-cucumbers
300 g (11 oz) coarse salt
750 ml (1¼ pints) white wine vinegar
a few heads of dill seed or a few sprigs of tarragon
100 g (3½ oz) very small pickling onions, peeled
2 cloves garlic

Wash and dry the gherkins as soon as possible, so they retain their freshness. Put them in a bowl and cover with the salt. Leave for 24 hours for the salt to draw out the water. The next day, drain the cucumbers and then rinse them in cold water. Drain and dry with a clean teacloth, and put them back in the washed and dried bowl.

Bring half the vinegar to the boil, simmer for 5 minutes then pour over the cucumbers. Cover with a clean cloth and leave in a cold place for 24 hours.

Strain the vinegar from the cucumbers, bring it to the boil and then set it aside until it is cold. Arrange the cucumbers in a glass jar, distributing the dill seed or tarragon, onions and garlic as you fill the jar. Pour over the cold boiled vinegar and top up the jar with the fresh vinegar. Cover with a waxed or plastic lid and store in a cold place for 2 months before opening.

GELÉE DE POMMES AUX HERBES

APPLE AND HERB JELLY

Early autumn apples, windfalls or even just apple peelings, make excellent apple jelly which can be flavoured with fresh herbs to make a delicious accompaniment or cold sauce for serving with roast game and gammon during the winter.

MAKES ABOUT 450 g (1 lb)

1 kg (2–4 lb) apples, washed and quartered, or
apple peelings
preserving or granulated sugar, warmed
1 lemon
a selection of fresh herbs: mint, chives, rosemary,
lavender, sage, juniper berries

Place the apples in a large pan with cold water to cover. Slowly bring to the boil then turn down the heat and allow to simmer for about 1 hour. Gently mash the fruit once or twice during the cooking.

Remove from the heat and cool slightly, then pour the contents of the pan into a jelly cloth (I use an old pillowcase) and suspend the bundle above a wide bowl to catch the drips. Leave for several hours, preferably overnight, until all the juice has dripped through. Do not be tempted to squeeze the bag or the final jelly will be cloudy.

The next day, measure the apple juice into the pan and bring to the boil. For every 500 ml (1 pint) of apple juice add 400 g (1 lb) of warmed sugar and stir over low heat until dissolved. Bring to the boil and cook until the temperature reaches setting point (105°C, 220°F), or when a teaspoon of jelly cooled on a saucer wrinkles when pushed with your finger. Add the lemon juice and remove from the heat.

Pour the apple jelly into several hot, dry jars and add the appropriate herbs to each jar.

CAREFUL SELECTION No French cook or chef would expect to buy any ingredient, particularly herbs, without thoroughly inspecting, feeling and smelling it to ensure the finest quality.

MINT JELLY Stir in finely chopped fresh mint and a drop of green food colouring.

CHIVE JELLY Make as for mint jelly replacing the mint with finely chopped chives.

ROSEMARY JELLY Add 2 or 3 sprigs of fresh rosemary to the jelly and stir well for 2–3 minutes or until the jelly is nicely flavoured. Remove the sprigs, stir in a drop of green food colouring and add a fresh sprig of rosemary to the jar.

LAVENDER JELLY Make as for rosemary jelly using fresh flowering spikes. Omit the colouring.

SAGE JELLY Make as for rosemary jelly.

JUNIPER JELLY Add 3 pounded juniper berries to each 150 ml ($\frac{1}{4}$ pint) of jelly.

Set the jellies aside to cool. Cover and label when they are quite cold.

INDEX

ACKNOWLEDGMENTS

The publisher thanks the following photographers and organizations for their permission to reproduce the pictures in this book:

Endpapers L'Espiquette fabric by Souleiado; 1 Jalain/Explorer; 2 Setboun/Rapho; 3 Pascal Chevalier/Agence Top; 6–7 C Bibollet/Agence Top; 9 Jean-Paul Dumontier; 10 P Hussenot/ Agence Top; 12–13 Christian Sarramon; 14 Retrograph Archive Collection; 16 Frederic/Jacana; 17 Lamontagne; 18 Viard/Jacana; 19 Lamontagne; 20–21 Christian Sarramon; 22 Nardin/Jacana; 23 Retrograph Archive Collection; 31 Jean-Paul Dumontier; 32 Georges Leveque (Creation de Jean Mus); 34 La Maison de Marie Claire (Duffas/Le Foll); 37 Georges Leveque; 43 J M Charles/Rapho; 45 Lamontagne; 52 Christian Sarramon; 56 Lamontagne; 58–59 Zefa Picture Library; 63 Charlie Waite/Landscape Only; 64 Errath/Explorer; 71 Fournier/Rapho; 75 Raymond de Seynes; 78 Mura/Jerrican; 81 La Maison de Marie Claire (Duffas/Le Foll); 84 Robert Opie; 87 Georges Leveque; 89 Delu/Explorer; 90–91 Thomas-Perdereau; 97 Noailles/Jacana; 102–103 Lamontagne; 106 Jean-Paul Dumontier; 111 Denis Hughes-Gilbey; 114 Larrier/ Rapho; 119 D Bouquignau/Agence Top; 120 Lamontagne; 124–125 P Hussenot/Agence Top; 130 R Mazin/Agence Top; 132 La Maison de Marie Claire (Duffas/Le Foll); 141 Goudouneix/Explorer; 145 Lerosey/Jerrican; 155 Remi Michel/ Rapho; 157 Chito/ANA/John Hillelson Agency;

Special photography by Linda Burgess; 13, 24–29, 40, 46–51, 55, 68–69, 76–77, 82–83, 94–95, 98–99, 108, 113, 116–117, 129, 134–139, 146–150.

The publishers would like to thank The Penguin Group for permission to include the recipe 'Calmars a l'Etuvee' from *Mediterranean Seafood* by Alan Davidson (Penguin Books, 1972, 1981) Copyright © Alan Davidson, and to thank Macmillan Inc. for permission to include the recipe for Stuffed Pumpkin from *Mastering the Art of French Cooking* Volume I, by Julia Child, Simone Beck & Louisette Bertholle. Copyright © 1961 by Alfred A. Knopf, Inc., a division of Random House, Inc.

The publishers would like to thank the following for their assistance: The Conran Shop, Fulham Road, London SW3; The Gallery of Antique Costume and Textiles, 2 Church Street, London NW8; Mrs Derek Gleeson and Mrs Gwen Tidball, Plymtree, Devon; Chris and Cathy Holbrey, Lowfield Organic Growers, Exelby, Bedale, Yorkshire; Hollington Herbs, Hollington Nurseries, Woolton Hill, Newbury, Berkshire; Sally St John Hollis, Welcombe Country Fayre, Darracott Farm, Welcombe, North Devon; Ann Lingard, Rope Walk Antiques, Rope Walk, Rye, Sussex; Nicolaus, Chenil Galleries, 181–183 Kings Road, London SW3; Norfolk Lavender, Caley Mill, Heacham, Kings Lynn, Norfolk; Tobias and the Angel, 68 White Hart Lane, Barnes, London SW3.

BIBLIOGRAPHY

Audot, L.E., *La Cuisinière de la campagne et de la ville*, 1818; Bardswell, Frances A., *The Herb Garden*, A.C. Black, 1911; Blandin, Charles, *Cuisine et Chasse de Bourgogne et d'ailleurs*, Editions Horvath, 1985 reimpression de l'edition de 1920; Bocuse, Paul, *The Cuisine of Paul Bocuse*, Granada, 1982; Boulestin, X. Marcel, *Herbs, Salads and Seasonings*, William Heinemann, 1930; Croze, Austin de, *Les Plats Regionaux de France*, Daniel Morcrette, 1928 reprinted 1977; David, Elizabeth, *French Country Cooking*, John Lehmann, 1951; Penguin Books, 1959; David, Elizabeth, *French Provincial Cooking*, Michael Joseph, 1960; Penguin Books, 1964; David, Elizabeth, *Spices, Salt and Aromatics in the English Kitchen*, Penguin Books, 1970; Davidson, Alan, *Mediterranean Seafood*, Penguin Books, 1972; Delaveau, Pierre, *Les Épices*, Albin Michel, 1987; Dumas, Alexandre, *Le Grand Dictionnaire de Cuisine*, Alphonse Lemerre, 1873; Fisher, M.F.K., *The Cooking of Provincial France*, Time Life, 1968; Fisher, M.F.K., *Two Towns in Provence*, Hogarth Press, 1985; Forot, Charles, *Odeurs de Forêt et Fumets de Table*, Seilc, 1975; Grigson, Jane, *Charcuterie and French Pork Cookery*, Michael Joseph, 1967; Penguin Books, 1970; Holt, Geraldene, *Budget Gourmet*, Hodder and Stoughton, 1984; Penguin Books, 1985; Holt, Geraldene, *French Country Kitchen*, Penguin Books, 1987; Lesbros, Mireille, *La Cuisine Traditionelle en Provence*, Le Regard du Monde 1985; Lowenfeld, Claire and Back, Philippa, *The Complete Book of Herbs and Spices*, David and Charles, 1974; Mabey, Richard, *The Complete New Herbal*, Elm Tree Books, 1988; Mazille, La, *La Bonne Cuisine du Périgord*, Flammarion, 1929; Médecin, Jacques, *Cuisine du comté de Nice*, Julliard, 1972; Penguin Books, 1983; Montagné, Prosper et Gottschalk, Dr, *Larousse Gastronomique*, Hamlyn, 1961; Montagné, Prosper, et Salles, Prosper, *Le Grand Livre de la Cuisine*, Flammarion, 1929; Pomiane, Édouard de, *Cooking with Pomiane*, Faber and Faber, 1962; Reboul, J.-B., *La Cuisinière Provençale*, Tacussel, 1895 reprint 1980; Rohde, Eleanour Sinclair, *A Garden of Herbs*, Herbert Jenkins, 1920; Root, Waverley, *The Food of France*, Macmillan, 1983; Serres, Olivier de, *Le Théâtre d'agriculture et mesnages des champs*, 1600; Stobart, Tom, *Herbs, Spices and Flavourings*, International Wine and Food Publishing Co., 1970., Penguin Books, 1977; Varenne La, *Le Cuisinier François*, 1651 edition reprint 1983, Bibliothèque Bleue; Willan, Anne, *French Regional Cooking*, Hutchinson, 1981; Zabar, Abbie, *The Potted Herb*, Weidenfeld and Nicholson, 1988.